SPEAK YOUR WAY TO SUCCESS

SPEAK YOUR WAY TO SUCCESS

**A Guide to Effective Speaking
in Business and the Professions**

ARTHUR W. SAGER
Executive Speech Consultant

McGRAW-HILL BOOK COMPANY

New York   San Francisco
Toronto   London   Sydney

PREFACE

This book on effective speaking for executives is designed specifically for leaders in industry and the professions. It may, however, be of even greater value to men who aspire to leadership. At no time in history has effective communication been more important to the man who wishes to advance his career. More and more decisions are reached in committees or by consensus. The man who can express his thoughts cogently and effectively enjoys a distinct advantage. He draws attention to himself; his thought is given respectful consideration. Furthermore, the spread of mass media has made listeners more critical of the form of expression. At the same time this spread has not lessened the vital importance of man-to-man or man-to-group confrontation.

The principles set forth in this volume have been developed through courses in speaking involving some eight thousand executives. These principles have been shaped and influenced by an impressive number of able and experienced men who have brought a wide and varied practical experience to the course sessions. They have been generous and effective in their suggestions and comments. These perceptive observations have kept the courses timely and dynamic. Hence the continuing success of the courses suggests that the techniques and suggestions which have benefited a substantial yet limited group will profit a wider range of actual and potential leaders.

In fact it is at the repeated suggestion of these men that this book is written. They urged that the basic principles, the characteristic attitudes, and the critical observations which form the core of the course sessions be assembled in written form. No formal text has ever been used in the courses; now it becomes evident that the courses themselves constitute a text. Insofar as it is possible to transform the oral to the written word, this volume attempts to supply that text.

The approach in this book is not didactic. There is no attempt to establish a rigid formula. The emphasis is directed toward the development of individual style, of an easy, direct, and informal manner, and of clear, emphatic presentation of ideas. The author recognizes that effective speaking is more often required in small groups—in committees, panels, department meetings—than it is in formal speeches. At the same time, more and more executives find that they must speak before large groups as representatives of their firm, their industry, or their profession. On these occasions the executive represents and personifies his firm or his profession. Hence it behooves him to carry his responsibility with some distinction. To assist him in this responsibility is the purpose of this book.

Arthur W. Sager

CONTENTS

ACKNOWLEDGMENT

I am deeply indebted to Mr. A. MacDonald Murphy of the faculty of Governor Dummer Academy for his invaluable help in preparing this book. His assistance in editing the text as well as constructive suggestions on the content are greatly appreciated.

Chapter 1
IT MUST BE SAID

How does oral communication stand in the world today? At first glance it would seem to occupy a minor position. The printing press has loosed a flood of material which clamors for the attention of the business or professional man. The daily papers, magazines, journals of opinion, books (both hardbound and paperback), trade and professional publications—all demand the attention of the man whose position in life requires him to be broadly informed on cultural, political, and economic matters yet, at the same time, to be abreast of the trends and movements within his own specialty. The mass of material which must be read to satisfy these two areas is formidable, and the task is time-consuming. As a result, most men have a constantly growing list of publications which they feel they must read—when they can find the time.

In addition, the formal press has an impressive rival in

duplicating machines. These devices produce an endless stream of reports, memorandums, interdepartmental communications, summaries, and announcements. If ignorance of the law is no excuse, neither is ignorance of paragraph 3 of Interoffice Communication 187 dated May 16. Yet the volume of paper flowing over the desk of a business or professional man makes it less and less certain that any one report or memorandum will be read as attentively as the writer had hoped. Indeed, many such communications are given only a cursory glance—just as professional journals are skimmed because time does not permit the attentive reading they deserve. The very ease by which the written word is spread detracts in some measure from its effectiveness.

Oral communication, then, has not lost its important place in the affairs of men. It is returning—if a return was ever really necessary—to a position of paramount importance. The President of the United States and the Prime Minister of Great Britain still find a face-to-face meeting the best way to work out a common policy. A State of the Union address by the President reaches more people directly than does the subsequent reporting of it. Both the formal speeches and the innumerable committee meetings of the United Nations provide safety valves to release international tensions which exchanges of notes might well strain to the danger point.

On the domestic scene—both in industry and in the professions—oral communications play a critical part. The importance accorded conventions in industry and colloquiums in the professions is clear evidence that the living word, produced by a warm human personality, has an effect which the printed word alone cannot supply. That effect is spread and intensified through the committee meetings and panel discussions which accompany these gatherings. Indeed business, science, and the learned professions are all putting emphasis on team projects, on decisions by consensus, on brainstorming, and on the stimulus which mind furnishes mind around a conference table. In the vital and delicate area of labor relations, the final compromise is normally worked out in the oral give-and-take around a conference table. Hence it appears that the ability to speak clearly, thoughtfully, and persuasively reaches its greatest usefulness on occasions of the greatest importance. The question remains, however, whether the ability to speak effectively is an innate talent or a skill. For if it is a skill, it can be learned.

The rather obvious answer is that it is both. Some men are born with a voice and presence which, coupled with a quick and penetrating mind, make them good speakers almost by instinct. These are the gifted few. For all except these, training and practice are necessary to develop even moderate skill. A man is not likely to qualify for the National Open after his first couple of weeks as a golfer. Two of the most sophisticated societies the world has known—the Greek and the Roman—were keenly aware of the need for training. To the Greek, the art of persuasion was one of the highest and noblest arts. He did not consider himself fully a man unless he took a serious and effective part in the debates and discussions on public and civic affairs. Since speaking was an art, he sought excellence in it. He made it an important part of his education, and he practiced it. In his mind it was inseparably bound with the study of psychology. Hence he developed superb skill in adjusting his style, his manner, and his subject matter to the group he was addressing.

From these Greek practitioners of the art, the Romans were quick to learn that the trained speaker could more than hold his own against the better endowed but untrained adversary in a discussion or debate. Both Cicero and Caesar took a postgraduate year in Greece to perfect themselves in rhetoric before returning to Rome to embark on their extraordinary careers. This year of study was the normal procedure for an ambitious young Roman. Caesar's technical skill—whether he was addressing the Senate or his troops, whether he was bringing a couple of rival political leaders to a compromise, or whether he was casting his spell over the unruly Roman mob—never failed him. Yet by nature he was not a speaker of the first rank.

The fact that the ancients in their highly literate and sophisticated society placed so much weight on training for effective speaking—on the art of persuasion— suggests that technique is also essential in the equally sophisticated and literate society of today. In all situations when consensus or agreement is desirable, persuasion plays a vital role. In the cockpit of ideas which a convention or conference represents, the man who understands how to present his ideas may make the decisive impression. And even in a departmental meeting among a group of close associates, the techniques of effective oral communication are still valid.

If, then, oral communication is an art with its special techniques, those techniques can be learned. They will not replace natural talent, but they will enhance it—will make the talent more sure. The easy yet forceful speaker will understand how he creates his effects and will employ these means more consciously. On the other hand, a feeling for technique will enable the less talented speaker to overcome some of the difficulties which would normally trouble him. He will understand how to make the most of his strengths and how to minimize the elements of his presentation where nature has not been generous.

In a very practical way this book will deal with oral communication. The illustrations will be drawn from the efforts of executives, scientists, and professional men in general as they sought to improve their ability to speak effectively. Their remarks will appear as they were actually delivered. They will be commented upon as though the critique were given at the conclusion of the speech. The purpose of the illustrations is to enable the reader to check his technique against that of able, intelligent men of varying natural ability. The principles which are illustrated apply to the experienced speaker as well as to the novice. A beginning golfer probably needs an extensive program of lessons, but even the professionals take lessons to correct weak spots in their technique. Long experience can make people careless about fundamentals which they once observed with great care. The principles and suggestions contained in the following chapters will serve as reminders to the experienced and as guidelines to the comparative novice. They are directed toward making oral communications better organized, clearer, more persuasive, and hence, more effective.

Chapter 2
PREPARING THE SPEECH

You have been asked to make a speech. This invitation may require you to address a convention, to speak at a dinner, or to talk to your local PTA. Whatever the occasion may be, you will be on your feet before a group of people who expect you to have something significant and stimulating to say. In a very literal sense you are subjecting yourself to an oral examination, for your audience will judge your competence in your topic by the substance and order of your ideas and judge you as a person by the way you present them. No sensible person goes into an examination without preparing himself thoroughly. Therefore, a speaker has a double motive for careful preparation: He will be judged both as an authority and as a person.

To Whom Are You Speaking?

How then should you begin your preparation? The first point to consider is the nature of your audience, for both what you have to say and how you say it will be influenced partly by the size of the audience, but fundamentally by its makeup. Audiences tend to fall into three broad divisions which have little to do with their size. The first of these is made up of people who you may assume have only a slight, superficial knowledge of your subject matter. The second consists of those who probably understand the basic concepts of your subject matter but who are in no sense expert. The third group is the exceptionally well informed, whose critical standards are high and who will demand the very best from a speaker. Therefore, what you must include in your talk and what you may safely take for granted will depend upon how well you estimate the frame of reference of your audience. Your decision in this respect will govern what technical terms you may use without explanation, what illustrations and examples will be appropriate, what references or citations you may make without laborious comment, what statistics or figures will be both relevant and informative. Since you are striving for a strong forward movement in the current of your ideas, you will try to avoid the swirls and eddies that too frequent explanations produce. So in determining at what level you should speak, you must strike a delicate balance between talking over the heads of your audience and talking down to them. Since an audience is offended when a speaker talks down to it, you are safer if you tend to raise your sights rather than lower them. The audience which has to stretch its mind a little is both attentive and complimented.

The manner in which you speak may also be influenced by the audience. Any large gathering usually indicates an occasion of some importance. The dignity of the occasion would prompt you to adopt a somewhat formal tone and attitude. However, the same degree of formality when you are addressing a group of colleagues would lead them to conclude that an invitation to speak had gone to your head. It takes skill and discrimination to find the right level for subject matter; it takes tact and sensitivity to strike the right tone and manner. In short, the personal relationship you establish with your audience determines how receptive it will be. The most effective channel of communication is kept open when the audience responds to the natural qualities of the speaker as a person, as well as to the speaker as a source of information.

The differences among audiences and approaches may be illustrated by the situation in which an automotive engineer finds himself. He has worked for a considerable time on the development of the gas turbine engine. He is asked to give two speeches on his specialty in the course of the same week—one at the weekly Rotary Club luncheon, the other at the annual dinner of the Midwest Association of Mechanical Engineers. On each occasion he will be expected to talk about gas turbines, yet his preparation for the two speeches will be entirely different. At the Rotary Club he will probably discuss the novel, the arresting features of the turbine and its significance for the future. His purpose is to be entertaining yet informative, and he will choose an easy, colloquial, informal manner. On the other hand, the association of engineers provides an audience of professionals, a group which at the same time can be highly critical and highly appreciative. Hence the speaker will try to produce as brilliant a technical exposition as he can. His tone and manner will be considerably more formal than they were at the Rotary luncheon. While the *general* subject for both these speeches is the same, the difference between the audiences is such that the preparation for one speech will be virtually no help in preparing the other.

An example of a situation which offers a speaker considerable leeway would be the following: The Secretary of State is asked to talk on American foreign policy. Obviously the topic lends itself to a variety of treatments and to a wide choice of specific topics. The Secretary may elect to talk on the currently critical area of foreign relations, on the philosophy underlying foreign policy during the past twenty-five years, on previous Secretaries who had a momentous effect on international relations, on the latest role of the United Nations, etc. Which topic he will choose will depend on his estimate of the interests and qualifications of the audience he proposes to address. A talk, for example, on the development of the Monroe Doctrine through various treaties might be of absorbing interest to the Foreign Policy Association; it would not be of the same interest to a convention of the Mid-West Building Trades Union. The two gatherings represent different levels of interest: the one highly technical, the other general. Hence, in preparing a speech, you must weigh carefully what your audience expects of you and what you may expect from your audience.

Developing Your Approach

Having assessed the nature of your audience, you can plan the approach to your topic. Your line of attack will depend upon the nature of your assignment. You may have been given a very specific subject; you may have a subject broad enough for you to select one aspect to develop; you may be asked to choose your own topic. Of course, even in the last instance you are probably expected to confine yourself to your generally recognized area of special knowledge. It is true that a complete change of pace is often refreshing, but if you are an authority on corporate tax structure and also an expert Alpinist, a talk on the three most dangerous climbs in North America might not be quite what an audience of bankers wants to hear. When you can choose your subject, or at least an aspect of it, you should give some thought to what will be of most interest to your specific audience.

But however restricted or however free in your topic, you should hesitate to settle too quickly upon your line of attack. Once you commit yourself to such a line, it is difficult to see other, perhaps more imaginative, possibilities. An overhasty commitment to your approach may lead to difficulties when you begin to organize your speech. Once your mind becomes set on a line of approach, it is difficult to change. As you work on your speech, you may think you are making improvements as you change and juggle details, but change in detail may not be enough. Your basic attack may be inferior. It will very likely be inferior if you have once set your mind to work on the obvious, the trite approach to your subject. A better course is to jot down on paper all the possibilities that occur to you. Give free rein to your fancy as it ranges over the topic. Many of these freewheeling ideas will not be practical, but some of them may beget others which will bring freshness and originality to your speech. Really creative thinking often consists in perceiving relationships between ideas or concepts which no one had observed before. By setting down a broad list of possible attacks on your subject, you may find a new grouping of ideas or a stimulating contrast. For example, the individual elements of Einstein's great equation were well known before he perceived the relationship the parts had to each other. It was his brilliant synthesis which brought him recognition. Furthermore, the synthesis or contrast you may make will arouse your own enthusiasm, for it will assure you that your treatment of the topic will not be hackneyed.

Enthusiasm for his own concepts is the best means a speaker has to arouse an answering enthusiasm in his audience. After all, an intelligent audience can hardly expect that all elements in your speech will be new to them. The best they expect is that their fund of information will be augmented in some details by what you have to say. Each person will select certain aspects of your talk to fill out his own background. But a fresh approach, if it can be managed, not only provides new information for the audience, but also casts a new light on the information they already have.

Concentrating Your Purpose

The third step in planning your speech is to consider your purpose or function in the light of your topic. What is your principal role to be? Essentially it may be _to describe_ a new product, a new process, a civic project, the effect of a specific act of Congress. Or your task may be _to explain_ a policy, a new concept, a technique, a decision on the part of management or of labor. Or you may be attempting _to persuade_ your audience. You may be defending or attacking the validity of a scientific theory, the appropriateness of a departmental reorganization, the merits of a new system, or the recommendations of the town finance committee. In most instances elements of each of these categories will be found in your speech, but also in most instances, one will be dominant. This is the one which will influence both your selection of supporting material and your manner of presentation. Each of these roles has its special techniques if it is to be effective in achieving its purpose. For instance, _description_ reflects your skill in relating things the audience knows to the new ideas you are presenting, or in finding a familiar but valid analogy. _Explanation_ also constrains you to be clear, but the stress is on orderly, sequential, logical flow of thought. _Persuasion_ forces you to take a second look at your audience. To what motives should you appeal? Is your argument to be directed to the mind or the heart? If to both, what should the proportion be?

The Time Factor

Your final act of preparation is to survey the time at your disposal. You must divide your time so that you can both gather material and then organize, compose, and polish your speech. Because you want to be as accurate and as informative as possible, you may be tempted to spend too much time in assembling the material you propose to organize. Of course you wish to draw on as rich a background as possible. No one is ever really satisfied that he has gathered enough facts, figures, citations, illustrations, or supporting anecdotes to do justice to his subject. But you must establish a cutoff time for yourself so that you have time to make the best use of your material. The fact that you do establish a form of time schedule will tend to force you to action. You will be less likely to put off the actual organization to the point that you have to rush the whole process. By setting a term to your period of assembling material, you can approach the problem of organization with a mind ready to concentrate on that important problem exclusively.

Chapter 3

ORGANIZING THE SPEECH

If your preparation has been sound, the organization of your speech may appear to be relatively simple. You have decided upon the tone and level of your remarks, you have gathered an ample body of material, and you are conscious of the time at your disposal. Now your only problem is to arrange that material so that it will have the maximum effect upon your audience. But this is not a simple task. Your organization requires great skill and judgment. An artist may have the finest canvas, the best pigments, even a brilliant concept, yet he may fail to produce a good painting. Having good material and a good idea is not enough. The design, the composition, is equally important.

Keeping an Eye on the Clock

Your first problem has to do with units of your speech. Obviously, you must first launch your topic, then develop it, and finally draw it to some sort of conclusion. Each of these parts presents its own internal problems, but the manner in which they are integrated into a balanced and graceful whole will make the speech succeed or fail. Too many speakers, for instance, fail to control their introductory remarks. They may extemporize on the remarks of the chairmen who introduce them. Then they try to work a transition between the extemporary and the prepared beginning and take much too long to do so. As a result they lack time to develop their major points adequately. Others err at the other end of their speeches by reaching their main point too soon; thus they end speeches not in a steady rise to a climactic point but in a flurry of anticlimactic observations. Both errors are the result of faulty organization.

Since time is the limiting factor in a speech, your best policy is to set a strict limit for each part. When you refuse to let one part steal time from another, you make certain that your speech will be in proportion. It will stand or fall as a unit. Furthermore you will select with greater care the material which time will permit you to include in each section. Hence, at this point, you should check the actual tempo at which you speak. Your natural and comfortable rate of speech will determine how much you can say in five minutes. If your delivery is to be warm and natural, it should not be rushed in an effort to encompass too much material in too little time. The effect you wish to create is that the time at your disposal and the substance of your remarks have been smoothly and perfectly matched.

A Spark at the Beginning

How do you begin? This question might be countered by asking another one: What are your aims in your introductory remarks? First, you wish to provide a spark to catch the attention and ignite the imagination of your audience. Television audiences who attend live shows are often submitted to a warming-up period. But your audience has not been conditioned for you; so you must awaken their interest by the vigor and freshness of your opening remarks. If you warm them up slowly you will have little time for the substance of your presentation. Second, your introductory remarks should suggest the purpose of your speech. Why is what you have to say important? What special significance has it to the audience you are addressing? Is its significance obvious, or must it be developed? Whatever device you have used to kindle the interest of your audience will probably help to suggest answers to these questions. But even though you have aroused the interest of your audience, that interest may die unless you at once establish the validity and pertinence of your subject. It is really a confession of weakness if you have to tell the audience that your topic is important. The importance should emerge from the structure of your introduction. In the process of introducing your subject it is perhaps better to show its importance rather than to tell the audience that what you have to say is significant. Finally, your introductory remarks should suggest both the scope and the limits of your presentation. Your time will unquestionably be too brief to permit an exhaustive treatment of your subject. However, the audience will not expect more than you promise to give them—if you have been careful to indicate the boundaries of your discussion. In most instances, a blunt statement is not the best means of indicating the phases of the topic you propose to cover. You can show both skill and grace in making the limitations clear, but not obtrusive.

A good beginning, then, should have a good deal of material done up in a small, neat package. It should present at once the best side of the speaker's personality, spur the interest and imagination of the audience, assure them that the topic is of immediate significance, and indicate what areas the speaker will discuss. Your skill will be reflected in your ability to compress these elements into a few minutes of speaking time without strain and without forcing the natural tempo of your speech.

Expanding Your Theme

The second major element—the development and expansion of your thought—also requires careful editing. In your preparation, hopefully, you have more or less saturated yourself in your subject matter. Both the information and the insights you have gathered from that information seem to be of major importance, yet you must discard a great deal in order to make an effective speech. To do so may seem like a painful amputation. But your audience is not in your position. They come to the topic without your rich background. They are not aware, nor should they be, of how carefully you are selecting from a wealth of related material. For that reason, a strictly limited number of points, each one adequately developed, will have a more powerful effect upon them than a rapid survey of all the points inherent in the topic. As a speaker, your dedication is to your subject matter and to the audience—not to your reputation as a savant or researcher.

In selecting the points you propose to develop, then, two criteria are helpful. The first is to select those aspects of your subject matter which will be most relevant to the audience you are addressing. You might decide, for instance, that a very important point is too technical for your audience. You would have to devote too much time to explanation and would risk losing your audience in the process. With another group that point should be used, because a very brief explanation would suffice and because the audience would appreciate that a difficult problem had been clarified for them. In general, too, the points you select should be arranged in a rising order of importance. As it proceeds, a speech should grow in strength rather than diminish. There is, however, one normal exception to this arrangement. The interest of the audience must be retained after the introduction has caught their imagination. For this reason, the first point you make should be both strong and interesting.

The second criterion in selecting and arranging your points is that they fit well together. Your preparation has given you a comfortably broad range of possibilities from which to choose. Some of these points will lend themselves to forming a coherent whole better than others, however valid they may be. Since you are thinking of the speech as a whole, even when you are organizing the parts, the principle of coherence should play an important part both in the selection and in the arrangement of material. Indeed the smooth, easy movement of thought from one major division of the speech to another and a similarly careful transition from point to point within the divisions should be your effort throughout the organization. You are successful when the audience feels that your flow of thought is obviously the clearest, most logical way to present the ideas you are advancing.

Finding the Right Support

A speech may present an ordered succession of well-chosen points. It may be coherent and may have effective transitions within the sections and between the sections. Yet it may be a very dull speech. It is dull because the support for each point is pedestrian.

In your organization, then, you should strive to illustrate your points with color, imagination, and variety. One point may be supported by an anecdote, a second by statistics, a third by analogy, a fourth by a citation. The nature of the supporting material will depend upon the subject matter, but how that material is used depends upon you. The points you make can seldom be original or arresting, but the imagination you bring to their support is the measure of your consideration for the audience. It may not be your purpose to entertain the audience; it is certainly not your duty to lull them to sleep.

You will find that restatement is an important principle in oral communication. A reader can always glance back at the text to remind himself of the points prior to the one engaging his attention. The audience must depend upon memory. The considerate speaker, then, will remind his audience of the progression of thought. If he is discussing the Christian virtues and has had considerable to say about faith and hope, he will mention these two virtues again before launching into his remarks about charity. Restatement need not be obtrusive. The ideas or points can be expressed in slightly different words. But skillful restatement keeps audience and speaker abreast of each other and puts a quiet emphasis on the speaker's line of thought.

The Summing-up

This emphasis obviously reaches its climax in the conclusion. This is the end toward which the speaker has been working since he first rose to his feet. It is the part of his speech that most of the audience will carry away with them. Since it is difficult to hold a climax, to be emphatic for too long, the conclusion should be brief. Ideally, it should be a perfect blend of words and matter —the purpose of the speech vividly revealed in terms the audience will remember. If that perfect blend cannot be achieved, the speaker should at least take special pains to be as clear and as vigorous as he can be and to choose his words with special care. One sentence too many, one weak or trailing phrase at the end, may spoil the whole effect. No one sentence in the whole speech should be composed with so much care as the last one.

Chapter 4
GETTING UNDER WAY

> Good beginning maketh good ending
> HENDYNGE

A good beginning may not necessarily make a good ending. But a beginning which performs its proper function will make a good ending likely. A poor beginning, on the other hand, may well spoil the effect of the speech as a whole. What then are the functions of the introductory portion of the speech?

In the first place you must catch the attention and interest of the audience, whether it be large or small. Most audiences in the beginning are disposed to be receptive to what you have to say, but their initial warmth will be quickly cooled unless you stimulate their imaginations at the outset. If your opening is dull, prosaic, hackneyed, they will probably conclude that the speech as a whole will follow the same pattern. They will condition themselves to endure rather than enjoy what you have to say. You must be sure, then, that your opening words will arouse rather than lull their interest. The stimulus you should provide is sometimes known as the "spark," and it can take various forms—forms which are limited only by your ingenuity and imagination.

Generating the Spark

One standard form is to make an arresting short statement: "The world's supply of petroleum has been exhausted." The reaction of the audience to such a bold announcement will vary from shock to open incredulity —but at least there should be a vigorous reaction. The speaker might then go on to say that thirty years earlier as a student at Atlantic University he had heard an eminent geologist declare flatly that the world's petroleum reserves would be exhausted in twenty-five years. He might then move to the essential purpose or theme of his talk, namely, that advances in technology and the explosion of knowledge had made a number of earlier predictions appear ridiculous. To be effective, an arresting statement should be brief, it should not trail off in a series of qualifying phrases, and it should apply directly to the theme or purpose of the speech. Thomas Paine's "These are the times that try men's souls" is a good example.

A second method of generating a spark is to use a quotation. While a very familiar quotation has the advantage in that its source and background are generally known, it has the disadvantage that your audience may assume that you will develop it in a conventional way. At the same time, a *short,* hackneyed quotation which you treat in an original, imaginative manner may be most effective. A trite quotation may be twisted or altered to provide a special effect; e.g., "To err is human, to forgive—costs the company money." But in using quotations you must remember that besides choosing one that is apposite, you must also consider the source. However general and appropriate the sentiments may be, a quotation from President Franklin D. Roosevelt is not likely to be sympathetically received by a group of conservative Republicans. The source of the quotation can arouse emotions which have nothing to do with its substance.

The quotation which begins this chapter is a convenient example of strengths and weaknesses in a quotation. Neither the wording nor the substance is original. The author, Hendynge, a shadowy figure from the age when the English language began, is not controversial. However, the antiquity of this citation may suggest that your problems in composing beginnings are not new ones. It has probably not been quoted frequently in the past. These are all factors in selecting a quotation which will stir the interest of the audience.

Still a third method of providing a spark is to ask a question or a series of questions. This method has some real hazards. It is very easy to ask questions which are so trivial or banal that the audience will at once begin to supply amusing and inappropriate answers. The audience will enjoy this process, but they will hardly take the rest of your speech seriously. The rhetorical question is an old and honored device, but it must be so worded that only one answer is possible. At the same time the form of the question and the area it explores should indicate the purpose of your discussion. A very ancient example, cited by Hamton Peterson in A *Treasury of the World's Greatest Speeches,* illustrates these points.

St. John Chrysostom is preaching on the fall of Eutropius, one of the emperor's most powerful ministers, who is cowering at the altar of the church where he has fled for sanctuary. He is in full view of the audience as Chrysostom speaks. Besides employing the rhetorical question with great skill, Chrysostom threw in a quotation for good measure:

> Vanity of vanities, all is vanity—it is always reasonable to utter this, but more especially at the present time. Where are now the brilliant surroundings of thy consulship? Where are the gleaming torches? Where is the dancing and the noise of dancers' feet, and the banquets and the festivals, where are the garlands and the curtains of the theatre, where is the applause that greeted thee in the city, where the acclamation in the hippodrome and the flatteries of spectators? They are gone, all gone. . . .

The list of questions continues with some comment between them. But it is worth taking a look at the questions.

The first question is somewhat general, but the succeeding ones are specific and concrete. Each one provides a vivid picture of one aspect of Eutropius' prosperity. Each of these aspects will be explored in detail during the body of the speech. By means of the questions, Chrysostom outlines the organization of his sermon. The quotation, on the other hand, establishes the tone and attitude which will characterize the whole discourse. Here the imagination is at once engaged, although the style would hardly be appropriate for a modern audience.

Still another method is to employ a short anecdote or narrative. If it is at all possible, you should make this a personal anecdote. Obviously in the narrative you should play the role either of victim or casual observer. However tempting the opportunity, you should never play the hero. If you do play the right role, you will introduce yourself to the audience as a modest, fallible, sympathetic person whose authoritative position on the platform has not gone to his head. The anecdote may be light or serious, but it must be appropriate to the tone and substance of your talk. Above all it must be short. The essence of a good narrative is that it must have concrete detail to stir the imagination of the listener. At the same time, detail is an attractive trap for the speaker, for it is easy to supply too much. Therefore, you must edit your narrative rigorously. If the anecdote is too much extended, your speech as a whole will be thrown out of proportion.

These four devices for providing a spark can be varied or combined in many ways which your ingenuity will suggest. But unless you are a born wit, you should generally avoid the stock "funny story" which so many speakers feel is an essential for an opening. Few of them are appropriate and fewer still are well told. If your audience has heard the story before, you are off to a very poor start. You owe the audience an original approach and one which will reflect your personality.

Introducing Your Purpose

In addition to providing a spark, the introduction should indicate the *purpose* or *theme* of your speech. What aspects of your topic do you propose to stress? Your topic is probably broad enough so that in the time at your disposal you cannot treat it exhaustively in all its aspects. The audience has no right to expect more than you promise to give them. But you should indicate the limits you intend to place upon your subject. Hence if your purpose is skillfully expressed, it will provide a subtle outline of the body of the speech which is to follow the introduction. Chrysostom used rhetorical questions to provide a spark, but these same questions indicated specific areas of human vanity which he proposed to decry. It is obviously better to establish the areas or limitations indirectly. You *can* say: "I promise this evening to discuss the Social Security system only as it applies to those who have made maximum contributions during their working lives." Here both the purpose and the limitations are clear, but the emphasis might be conveyed more gracefully.

You show greater skill when you let the audience discover your purpose through suggestion. They are flattered by the appeal to their intelligence. Since it is also helpful to relate your topic directly to the interests of the audience, you might say: "Most of you have paid maximum Social Security taxes ever since you came under the system. You belong to a small but interesting minority." Here you express the thought contained in the bald statement, but you are both personal and indirect, as well as being clear.

Choosing an Attitude

The last phase of your introduction which you must consider is the tone or *attitude* you are to assume. Are you essentially conveying information? Are you persuading your audience to adopt a point of view? Are you advocating a course of action? Are you attacking a decision or a projected plan? Are you simply entertaining? Whatever attitude your topic demands should be established in your introduction, your tone—and tone includes both diction and style—must be appropriate to the topic and to your attitude toward it.

As You Might Begin

Perhaps the best way to see how these principles work in practice is to examine some actual speeches. These examples were recorded on tape during classes in speaking for executives. They were prepared by bankers, industrialists, editors, and scientists who were speaking without notes. The requirement that they not have notes was to discourage them from memorizing their speeches. A speech that has been memorized word for word usually lacks ease and spontaneity of delivery. Concentrating on a feat of memory, the speaker loses touch with his audience; he may appear to be reading to them rather than carrying on one side of a warm and active dialogue.

These introductions have not been edited. However, in all fairness it must be said that they sounded much better than they appear in print. They were chosen because they are introductions which do represent the strengths and weaknesses which also appear in longer and more formal speeches. It is a salutary experience for you to have a short speech recorded on tape and subsequently transcribed. You will learn the difference between what you thought you said and what the audience heard.

The first example of introductory remarks is taken from a speech entitled "Teach Your Child to Type." It was given by a senior editor of a publishing house, who is an experienced and distinguished speaker:

> How many of you have a child, for whom you feel some degree of affection or responsibility, in grades 3, 4, 5, or 6? Are you concerned with that child's progress in school? How many of you have a typewriter in your home? Having that typewriter gives you the means of helping that child leap forward *an extra half year* in spelling, word knowledge, and reading—the heart of the intermediate grades. You should know a few things about typing and pre-teeners.

This introduction has many merits. By employing the rhetorical question, it establishes a bond between the speaker and those who can make an affirmative reply to the first question. The third question ties together the two aspects of the topic—the child and the typewriter. The final statement is effective in establishing both the *purpose* of the speech and the *limits* of the topic. Adults and teen-age students are excluded. The editor then went on to offer cogent evidence, based on his own experiments, of the notable improvement in reading and writing on the part of children who had been taught to type.

On the other hand, there are minor weaknesses in this introduction. Some remark about the general interest in education might have caught those who have no children in the suggested age bracket. The second question —"Are you concerned with that child's progress in school?"—opens the door to a flippant answer. Perhaps a rephrasing—"How deeply," or "How genuinely"—would have brought the question into harmony with the general tone. A transitional device, a *yet* or a *but* would throw the third question into sharper contrast with the first two. As it stands, it is somewhat bald. These observations suggest that attention to key words is necessary to give even the best of technical devices their full impact.

The second example of the beginning of a speech is taken from a talk, "Supervisors in Action," given by the vice-president of a large metropolitan bank. It provides a good illustration of what can happen when a speaker fails to exercise firm control over his address as a whole.

> Tonight I'd like to talk to you gentlemen about supervisors in action. Everywhere we look today, whether we realize it or not, we have people supervising other people—whether it be on a farm in Idaho, a textile plant in South Carolina, an insurance company in Hartford, Connecticut, a superhighway in Ohio, even at Mammoth Trust in New York City. The job classifica-

tions of people who supervise in that bank run the full gamut from assistant section heads, section heads, group heads, up through officer levels, even up to and including the president of our bank. Perhaps the most important thing we should consider is what makes a supervisor, and maybe more importantly, what can we do to become more effective supervisors. Many studies have been made about the subject—none of them have been conclusive. However, there have been basically three judgments, we'll call them, arrived at which call a supervisor a successful one. First, a supervisor must know what his employees think of him; secondly, he must know what his superior thinks of him; and thirdly, he must know what he thinks of himself. This, then, goes into what we might call the successful supervisor.

Here the speaker intended to start with a strong initial statement. But the first sentence does not fit that category. In fact it should be omitted entirely. The second sentence might do if the specific examples were put in a separate sentence which would expand and define the short, emphatic statement. However, what follows the initial statement is a mass of wordy and repetitious generalizations. No authority, for instance, is cited for the studies of effective supervision, and although these studies are termed inconclusive, three rather firm conclusions are drawn. The speaker seems to promise his audience that each of these conclusions will be developed in the body of his speech. Actually he failed to do so.

In the beginning of this speech the spark is so dim as to be almost obscured; the purpose is hidden in the subordinate clause, "which calls a supervisor a successful one"; and the scope or limit of the speech is not realized in practice. Here the organization of the speech as a whole and of its component parts was faulty. The poor organization of the beginning, which is too long under the circumstances, threw the speech as a whole out of proportion and was partly responsible for difficulties which occurred later on. The speaker, for instance, did not conclude on the issue which was presented so obscurely in the beginning.

The final example represents the effective use of a quotation combined with a question. It comes from a speech on the federal war on poverty which was given by another editor of a large publishing house.

> Senator Miller of Iowa, in a recent campaign speech, asked the question: "Since it costs more to keep one student in a Job Corps camp for one year than it does to keep one student at Harvard for a year, are your tax dollars being spent properly?" This is a question that is being asked by many people across the country as they try to evaluate the effectiveness of our war on poverty that was put into effect by the federal government some years ago. I think that before we can make an objective decision as to whether it has been a success or not, we should evaluate the two major agencies charged with the responsibility of conducting the war on poverty. These two are, first, the MBTA training program and, second, the Job Corps program.

This is a very sound beginning. The authority cited should carry weight since he must have been present when the programs were debated in Congress. The fact that the quotation is in the form of a question engages the interest of the audience because they are asked to collaborate with the speaker in finding an answer. Furthermore, the substance of the question has a direct appeal to the audience—any argument directed to the pocketbook arouses a personal response. Then, having suggested that the topic is of more than local interest, the speaker at once established the limits of his discussion—the two agencies whose effectiveness he proposed to examine.

In a relatively short time he fulfilled the criteria for a good beginning. He provided a spark, he established his purpose—an evaluation of the poverty program—and he limited his discussion to two important agencies. The one slight flaw was his assuming that the audience understood what MBTA stood for. A check revealed that less than a fifth of his audience did know what the abbreviation meant. But this well-organized introduction did lead to a well-supported comparison of the two agencies in the body of his speech and to a firm and logical conclusion at the end.

The importance of a good introduction can hardly be exaggerated. If you can provide a spark which will at once catch the imagination of your audience, you have begun to ensure the success of your speech. If you can make both your purpose and the scope of your discussion clear to your audience, you will make the rest of your speech a mutual endeavor which will give pleasure and satisfaction both to you and to them. As Aristotle remarked in his *Poetics* [1]: "*To be learning something is*

[1] Richard McKeon, *Introduction to Aristotle*, Modern Library, Inc., New York.

the greatest of pleasures, not only to the philosopher but also to the rest of mankind."

Finally, it is well to remember that the introduction serves to whet the appetite, not to satisfy it. Hence the beginning of your speech should be as short as you can make it while satisfying the conditions for a good introduction. It must be in proportion to the whole speech so that you will have ample time to develop in sufficient detail the topics you have selected for discussion.

Chapter 5
DEVELOPING YOUR THEME

You now come to the most important part of your speech—the middle part. Here the points which you have chosen to discuss are developed in detail. Here the force of your explanation, persuasion, or advocacy is brought to bear on the minds and emotions of your audience. It is the section of your speech which must satisfy the expectations you have aroused through your introduction. In this section you validate the purpose you suggested in your beginning, and you lay the groundwork for a logical and acceptable conclusion. Indeed this segment is so important that it will normally consume about two-thirds of the time at your disposal.

Your Points and Their Order

If your organization has been careful, you have already selected those aspects of your topic—the points—which you propose to advance or establish. You have kept in mind that to explain a difficult concept to your audience or to offer them persuasive evidence may take time. The more expert you are in your field, the more you must guard against taking for granted that the audience is familiar with the basic concepts in that field. Therefore, two or three well-developed points may have a more powerful impact than four or five which are only partially developed or which assume information which the audience does not possess. Just as you weighed the makeup of the audience and the nature of the occasion in organizing your speech, so you must bear these same factors in mind as you develop your thought in detail. Even if one of your points must cover somewhat familiar ground, your supporting material may be sufficiently fresh and imaginative that the point may seem new to the audience.

Whatever number of points you may choose to develop, you still must decide their order. The last point you make ought to be the one which will have the greatest impact on the audience. Certainly it is the one which they are most likely to carry away with them. But here again imagination is called for. As an expert you may know that one point is of prime importance, yet its technical nature might prevent a general audience from grasping that importance. Hence you might choose for the climactic spot a point with a more subjective appeal. You would not necessarily, then, use the same final point in a speech to a group of highly informed people that you would use in addressing a general audience. A tennis player counts on his best shot to score important points, but his best shot is not necessarily the same one against all opponents. Likewise your final point will be dictated by your appraisal of your audience.

On the other hand the point which comes right after your introduction is also important. If your introduction has roused your audience to a high pitch of expectation, you had better satisfy that expectation at once. When you carry their interest into the body of the speech, you have established a momentum which should sweep forward to the end. Of course *all* the points you choose to develop should be important, but some are likely to have more immediate interest than others. So the effect on the audience and the method by which you propose to develop each point are important in establishing the order in which each one is presented. For instance, an initial point supported by a liberal use of statistics might chill a general audience, whereas it might fascinate a group of bankers. The same point supported by a brief anecdote might catch the imagination of the general audience, while the bankers might suspect that you were about to waste their time with a watered-down presentation. Any technical discussion directed toward a general audience should probably lead them gently into the more difficult concepts, but a scientific audience should at once be given an arresting aspect of your theme. Therefore the type of audience you are addressing should be a major influence as you determine the order of your thought.

Factors other than audience reaction will also affect the order of your points. There are some standard methods of ordering thought which may prove helpful to you as you expand your theme as a whole. One of these is *time*. This approach is conventional; but if chronology is inherent in your material, you should at least consider this order. Moving against the clock is fraught with hazards for writer and speaker alike. Failure to follow time order almost always offends against clearness—one of the principal virtues of a speech. Similar to *time* order is *place* order. This order is not so common in a speech, but if your points apply to physical motion of some kind, your audience must be aware of the direction and extent of movement. In discussing some problem of the Middle East, you will help your audience if your comments follow a physical direction. Not everyone can make the leap from Iran, to Aden, to Lebanon, with complete assurance that he knows just where he is.

Your points may also be arranged in a *cause to effect*, or an *effect to cause* order. In choosing either one of these, you should consider whether your points represent a process of analysis or of synthesis. If you were to discuss automation as it affects banking, you might choose either method, depending upon the thrust of your theme. Your approach might be to accept automation as established and to demonstrate some of its significant effects or to reverse the process by showing the causes which influenced banks to adopt automation. Realizing what process you are employing will assist you in arranging your points in a clear and forceful order.

Closely related to the cause-effect relationship is the *general to specific* or *specific to general* order. This order adapts itself well to speakers, and it has proved authority. Plato remarked that nothing was more important to clear thought than knowing whether you were moving to a general conclusion or away from one. Hence if you are advocating the development of a new product, you would move from specific and varied evidence to a general statement that the new product will be both advantageous and profitable. By keeping in mind the principle you are employing, you will avoid placing the general statement between two bodies of specific evidence. This error reduces the second body of evidence to weak afterthoughts.

The value of these conventional systems or of others you might use, such as a series of questions, is that they make you conscious of precisely what you are doing. So you avoid starting one system of development then unconsciously shifting to another. Any systematic order can be varied. What is important is that you are aware of what you are doing so that your variations are conscious, not inadvertent.

Audible Means of Support

A number of ways by which to develop and support your individual points are available to you. By taking advantage of this variety of means, you can make less obvious the overall system by which you have ordered your points and at the same time lend color and freshness to your speech. For by concentrating all your attention on *what* you are going to say, to the exclusion of *how* you are going to say it, you may unconsciously develop all your points in much the the same way. Thus unless you label them plainly as *first, second, third,* or *in the first place, next,* they may not be clearly differentiated in the minds of the audience. They may tend to merge into a general composite statement. However, by making the effort to present each point in a different manner, you impress each one on the audience and also keep their original interest and expectation high. There are a great many ways in which you can expand, develop, and support your points. Like the devices for catching the attention of the audience at the beginning of a speech, they can be modified or combined as your own imagination and ingenuity suggest. You should simply bear in mind that a form of development which will have an immediate and powerful appeal to one type of audience will have little or no appeal to another type.

One of the oldest and most trustworthy ways of developing a point is through *analogy.* By working out a somewhat detailed comparison between the concept you are advancing and the concept which must be familiar to most of your audience, you can produce in their minds a sense of sudden and complete illumination. Because it contains concrete references, an effective analogy is easy to remember; it often brings an abstract idea down to earth and fixes the point in the audience's memory. The parables in the Bible furnish an excellent illustration of the force of analogy. People who have forgotten much of what they learned in Sunday school still remember the parables vividly. Writers and speakers refer to them with perfect confidence that their readers or audiences will at once grasp the signficance of the reference.

To be most effective the analogy should fit several aspects of the concept you are attempting to make clear. Otherwise it becomes a simple metaphor or simile. You might, for instance, be developing the point that in business and government alike there must be clear-cut areas of responsibility and authority. To do so you might borrow the well-known analogy from Shakespeare's *Henry V*. You might quote it directly or paraphrase it in part or as a whole:

Therefore doth heaven divide
The state of man in divers functions,
Setting endeavour in continual motion:
To which is fixed, as an aim or butt,
Obedience: for so work the honey bees,
Creatures that by rule of nature teach
The act of order to a peopled kingdom.
They have a king and officers of sorts;
Where some, like magistrates, correct at home,
Others, like merchants, venture trade abroad,
Others, like soldiers, armed in their stings,
Make boot upon the summer's velvet buds,
Which pillage they with merry march bring home
To the tent-royal of their emperor;
Who, busied in his majesty, surveys
The singing masons building roofs of gold,
The civil citizens kneading up the honey,
The poor mechanic porters crowding in
Their heavy burdens at his narrow gate
The sad-eyed justice, with his surly hum
Delivering o'er to executors pale
The lazy, yawning drone. I this infer
That many things, having full reference
To one consent, may work contrariously.

Here you are in a position to draw not a single comparison, but a whole series of parallels. Some such analogy would match your original contention at more than one point and so produce a multiple effect. But you must remember that a false analogy, however spectacular it may be, will do you more harm than good. Your audience will rightly suspect you of being more interested in producing an effect than in being clear and logical.

Closely allied to analogy is the *illustrative story* or *anecdote*. This will expand and develop a point by showing how some one aspect of the general topic worked out in a specific instance, how it was first discovered or first utilized, or how it met an unusual situation. If the story provides firsthand experience or observation, it will have a strong appeal to the audience. Everyone is flattered and impressed when he gets information from the source itself. A speaker who can furnish an audience with a sense of participation in an event, even at one step removed, will find members of the audience repeating his story for a long time afterward. As they remember the anecdote, so they will remember the point, too. But if your personal experience does not provide you with a suitable anecdote, you may still draw on the experience of others. You must simply be sure that the anecdote bears *directly* on your point and is not included simply because it is a good story. The accounts of George Washington's cutting down the cherry tree and Abraham Lincoln's walking miles to return 2 cents in change to a customer of his New Salem store are both hackneyed and probably apocryphal, yet countless speakers have used them to support their points. If stale and doubtful anecdotes can produce some effect, a lively and original story is likely to make a strong impression.

Since each age, and indeed every area of human endeavor, has its own men of distinction, you might cite from the life or experience of a leader in your field or of a person generally known to the public. Contemporary biography is a flourishing aspect of publishing, and magazines publish both profiles and articles which evaluate contemporary figures. Books and magazines are excellent sources of illustrative anecdotes, but here again you must be selective. You will hurt rather than advance your cause by citing a story most of your audience has already seen in *Reader's Digest*. Originality, freshness, appropriateness are the qualities you are seeking in your anecdotes. In addition, whatever story you select must be one which makes its point very quickly. However appropriate it may be, it should be rejected if it requires an elaborate buildup. Furthermore, its purely illustrative role should be apparent. Unless you exercise firm control, a good story can overshadow and even obscure the point you are making. It is the point, not the story, you want the audience to remember.

Still another method of establishing a point is by *definition*. It is easy to see that the precise, intelligible definition of a technical or scientific term in itself might be enough to authenticate a point in the eyes of a lay audience. Indeed it is essential that all such terms be made perfectly clear when you suspect that a part of your audience may not be informed, even though these terms may be the commonplaces of your field of knowledge. But terms other than technical ones are often most in need of definition.

Words such as *liberal, conservative, humanitarian,*

progressive, democratic mean entirely different things to different people. *Democratic* is a good example. To people in the non-Communist world it connotes the right to disagree, the right to be in a minority, the existence of at least two political parties. In the Communist world, however, *democratic* denotes the party of the people; hence, in the eyes of that world, any other party would of necessity have to be in opposition to the people—a minority would ipso facto be subversive and without rights. A state with a single party is the core of the definition. Thus people on opposite sides of the Iron Curtain have diametrically opposed concepts when they employ the term *democratic*. But even on this side of the Curtain, the word is understood in different ways. For some, *democratic* means that all issues must be decided by majority vote; others maintain that delegation of authority is an essential part of the democratic process.

This example suggests that it is every bit as important for you to define key abstract terms as it is to define key technical terms. Failure to define a technical term may well neutralize a point you wish to stress. The audience may simply not follow your discussion because they do not understand one or two words. But failure to define an abstract term may cause different groups in the audience to follow tangential paths of thought into areas from which you cannot collect them again. Once you have established a definition, you bind the audience to the limitations you have set up.

Statistics

Some points require the support of *statistics* and purely *factual information*. Statistical evidence, facts, and figures provide the only means of validating certain general statements. If you are an accountant, a banker, or a scientist, this type of evidence is of absorbing interest and significance. You can grasp the essential data, estimate the authority of the source, and instantly relate the material to the point at issue. But for a general audience statistical or factual support may have to be more selective and may require more explanation. Figures may speak for themselves, but they speak a different language to the informed and the uninformed. Hence the impact on your audience produced by this mode of development will likely depend upon quality and selectivity rather than quantity. If several of your points demand this type of evidence for their support, you should seriously consider the use of a visual aid. By this means, the facts and figures are kept before the eyes of your audience, who do not have to catch them as they fly from your lips.

Citations

Again the point you are making may best be supported by the authority of others. Even the most radical and controversial topic can be fortified by *citations* and *supporting statements*. This is the method of development commonly employed by lawyers, scholars, and political speakers. It can be dull and pedantic—but it need not be. It becomes dull only when you cite from pedestrian or hackneyed sources. A little extra effort on your part can produce fresh and stimulating opinions and statements. You may find support in an unexpected source—even from the ranks of those who might be expected to hold a contrary opinion—or the citation may be arresting in itself. But your audience will be affected also by your good judgment in selecting authorities. Since the real experts in a given field are often known only to their fellows, you may choose to cite better-known even though less technically eminent, personages to a general audience. The opposite procedure would hold if you address a group from your special field. Since such a special group will have varying opinions about the authorities you quote, you must be careful to use one expert to bolster another. A name representing a different point of view may close the ears and minds of part of your audience; so you may have to use a second or third name to open them again. However, like the anecdote, the citation can easily be too long. Try to find passages which support your point in a very few sentences. Sometimes a supporting statement is so apposite and so well worded that you will hesitate to cut it. If the citation is long, you should summarize it. Quotations which go on too long, as well as too many quotations, drive the point you are making out of the minds of the audience. You must not be dwarfed by allies you summon to assist you. Keep your supporting statements crisp, varied, and subordinate.

Other means

There are other devices for expanding the points you make in the body of your speech. Used in moderation, *paradox* is likely to have an immediate effect on your audience. The resolution of the apparent contradiction will alert their imaginations. The philanthropist who says that his most cherished possessions are the things he has given away, or the military figure who declares that war is the shortest road to peace, is making use of *paradox* to arrest attention and to lead into a detailed explanation. An occasional paradox, especially if it is placed at a point where you feel the audience should be stimulated, will provide an effective change of pace.

You should remember, too, that *metaphors* and *similes* serve the same purpose as *analogy*, but they achieve their effect in smaller space. A metaphor, you will recall, is a comparison which does not employ *like* or *as*. People speak of someone as a "snake in the grass" or a "bull in a china shop," not literally, but by way of comparison. A simile expresses a comparison: "The speech was as long as a weekend in the country to a New Yorker."

Aristotle said that skill in metaphor is the truest mark of genius. He meant, doubtless, that it is the most perceptive mind which sees relationships and similarities between apparently disparate objects and situations. Metaphor lies in the heart of the imagination. When it is well used, it can pass into common speech. Churchill's metaphor of the Iron Curtain became commonplace at once, as did Grantland Rice's reference to the Four Horsemen. *Simile,* in which the comparison is stated rather than implied, is a little less subtle but almost as effective as metaphor.

All these devices, whether used singly or in combination, will suggest others to you. But each point you make should have some concrete illustration or development for the audience to remember in connection with that point. Here again, however, you must maintain a sense of proportion. A general statement buried under a mass of detail, illustration, or citation is no more effective than an unsupported statement. Except for statistics, one or two *good* illustrations or citations are better than three or four. If you must err, it is better to err on the side of economy rather than of profusion.

Finally, the points must be linked together. There should be a smooth, easy, logical, and reasonably rapid flow of thought from point to point. You must, then, be conscious of your transitions as you order your points and as you develop them. If your speech contains several points, you should consider the advisability of *restatement*. This device reminds the audience of the progress that has been made and of the stage the speech has reached. You might, for instance, be speaking of the effect of taxation on the workingman. To introduce your third point you might say, "in addition to federal and state taxes, there are purely local taxes." This transition also acts as a *restatement*, for it reminds the audience of the two previous points, and it suggests that the third may also be the last. Transitions can be managed more inconspicuously than the *first, second, third* method. Words such as *next, on the other hand, moreover, furthermore, consequently,* and *in addition* can carry the thought from one point to the next. A more subtle method is to repeat a key word used at the conclusion of one point in the first sentence of the succeeding point— "He *proposed* that the following steps be taken: the number of troops in Germany be reduced by 10 percent, dependents of servicemen be returned to the United States, and the number of military establishments in Germany be reduced. This *proposal* aroused heated objections." The word is enough to carry the audience across the division in thought. You must have bridges, not stop signs, between the divisions of your speech.

By turning to some actual talks recorded in public speaking seminars for executives, it is possible to see how well or how poorly points are developed by intelligent, and in many cases practiced, speakers. Remembering that these talks are transcribed directly from tape, but that they are not impromptu speeches, you will observe that good intentions and native ability are not always enough to develop points effectively. You will probably see that both preparation and practice are essential to a good speech.

The first example is taken from a speech given by the vice-president of a large New York corporation. His theme involves certain abuses, as he sees them, in the welfare state. He is concerned with what he considers to be the rapidly increasing, misdirected paternalism of government and with the effect it may have on both individuals and the nation. He develops his points by employing a personal anecdote, a concrete example, and an analogy in that order.

A friend of mind said to me recently, "Why don't you come up and visit me in my cottage in the Maine woods?"

"Well," I said, "that would be lovely. I'd like to do that." And I said, "I didn't know you had a cottage in the Maine woods!"

And he said, "I don't. But," he said, "when Congress passes the guaranteed annual wage, I'm going to sell my home here. I'm going up to Maine. I'm going to build a cottage in the Maine woods. I'm going to send my kids to school at the expense of the government." And he said, "since you'll be working for me, if you want to come up about twice a year and get gassed up," he said, "that's all right with me."

Well this started a train of thought in my mind, and it occurred to me, you know we talk about the forgotten man in this country—in the 1920s it was the farmer; in the 1930s it was the wage earner; in the 1940s it was Alf Landon; in the 1950s I suppose it was Betty Grable. In the 1960s maybe it's the income-producing man and corporation, because after all, where is all this governmental largess to come from except from the man who works with the corporation which produces the wealth? And yet we hear very little about them. We hear about the culturally disadvantaged. We hear about the unfortunate victims of society. We hear about the civil rights of the criminal. We hear very little about the rights of his unfortunate victims.

Sometimes I think we really don't have to wait for 1984. Maybe the age of new things is already upon us. A few years ago, not too many years ago in fact, in the city of Newburgh, New York, they had a city manager who was pilloried and driven from public life because he came up with the revolutionary idea that perhaps the recipients of public welfare in his city should be required to work for the commonweal and do a day's work for a day's income.

Sometimes it strikes me that we're at the same point that the Roman Empire was about the beginning of the fifth century. We still send our legions out to fight the barbarians on our shrinking perimeters, but the legions that we send out have to support a larger and larger group of camp followers. Our gladiators still come back from the fray, but instead of being presented with olive leaves and palm fronds, they are greeted with suggestions that perhaps it would be just as well if they didn't show up at the Circus Maximus because, after all, their presence might be a bit depressing to the voluptuaries there. Well, all civilizations have their end, and perhaps ours is no exception. Personally, I'd like to see it go on a little bit longer. I think it's a pretty good civilization. And the question is what can we do about it?

Here a strong point of view is presented, and the speaker has used a variety of means to support aspects of the thesis which he wishes to advance. The major weakness here is insufficient preparation. The anecdote in the first paragraph has not been worked over so that it could be presented in fewer words and with more point. The repetition of *I said* and *he said* is doubtless unconscious, but it does indicate the price you pay when you fail to exercise conscious control over your words when you speak. Practice would have removed this difficulty and would have revealed that the anecdote needs a stronger climax. Another slight indication of hasty preparation is the inclusion of Betty Grable among the forgotten men, a position she would abhor on two counts. This development does, however, return vigorously to the speaker's theme.

There is no transition between the first and second points. The reference to George Orwell's *1984*, good as it is, needs to be tied more directly to the specific example cited in the paragraph; otherwise the audience may miss the allusion. As it is presented, it might simply be a date. Since the point of this paragraph is also to be drawn by inference, more careful preparation would have suggested that either the beginning or the end be made more explicit.

The third point, developed by analogy, is introduced in almost the same words as the second point. These might be transitional, except that a conscious transition would probably involve a stronger word than *sometimes*. However, the analogy itself is sound, although lack of preparation and rehearsal shows up in the confusion between gladiators and legionnaires. This may seem to be a small distinction, but for anyone who is aware of it, the analogy collapses.

Since this speech had a conclusion, it is an admirable example of a varied and imaginative development of a thesis spoiled in part by haste in preparation and by lack of practice. It should reinforce the observation that talent and perception can carry a speech just so far. To remove the rough edges, careful organization and adequate practice are essential for most speakers.

Another example of a short, prepared speech is one given by an officer of a New York bank. He is attacking a proposal that New York State conduct a lottery in aid of education. After his introductory remarks, he seems to base his objections to the proposed law on the contention that it is both impractical and unethical. He supports the first of these contentions by an analogy strengthened by statistics, the second by a citation.

Only a few years ago, the state of New Hampshire took similar action, and already the voters of that state are starting to reconsider their actions. A number of towns and cities within the state had an amendment on their ballots this year to decide whether or not they would continue the use of this lottery. And well they might when you reexamine the results of the lottery over the past two years. In 1964, for instance, the initial year of the lottery, the gross income was 5.6 million dollars and the amount received by the school districts in the state was 2.6 million dollars. In subsequent years the gross receipts from the lottery have diminished, and as a result, in the three years that it has run—1964, 1965, 1966—the total amount received by school districts in the state of New Hampshire was 7 million dollars, or approximately 56 dollars per pupil. Now, it's not important that gambling be involved in a lottery. It seems to me that gambling is a human vent that is as old as history and undoubtedly will survive civilization. What is important is the fact that the lottery is the panacea for all of the problems in the involvement of improving and expanding education in the state.

I think that the comments made in the *Weekly Bond Buyer* express my sentiments on this subject particularly well. "When a public government lowers itself to a lottery to raise money that should be raised straight-forwardly by taxes, how much lower can it stoop? "The money needs must come overwhelmingly from the underpropertied masses, the very people who are in the most need of the community's help. It is no overstate-ment to insist that a state lottery means hustling the civil service bureaucracy into the financial ghettos to pick the pockets of the poor."

Here the means employed to develop the two points are basically sound. The analogy between one state and another is appropriate and authoritative. The use of statistics is judicious. They weigh strongly in support of the point of impracticality, and they are few and simple enough to be easily remembered. At the end of the para-graph the speaker seems to be making the distinction between moral and ethical conduct, a distinction which is to lead to his next point. That point may be inferred from his well-selected citation, but the speaker needs more than an inference to establish a major point. He should not have depended on the citation by itself to speak for him. Some comment or interpretation is re-quired from the speaker, especially since his conclusion should pull the two points together in a strong restate-ment of his theme.

In this brief speech more time should have been de-voted to the actual wording. We are asked to reexamine the results of the lottery over the past *two* years. We are then given the result for *one* year. When comparative figures appear, they are for *three* years. These are small details, but they may well disturb some members of the audience. Another place that demands more attention to wording is the final sentence in the first paragraph. As the sentence which concludes one point, it should be clear, vigorous, forceful; yet it drifts into a succession of abstract polysyllables. Here again is an instance of sound and varied organization and development marred by failure to carry out in detail an excellent intention. Again, polish and practice could easily remove the imperfections.

The next speech provides an example of a very well-organized one in which each of several points is supported by facts and figures. The support is apposite and convincing, but had there been more contrast in the development of the issues, the speech would be livelier. The speaker, a magazine editor, began by asking questions about publishing a magazine. How do you decide on editorial content? How is the advertising sold? Who buys advertising and why? And who will buy the magazine, and will they read it? The structure of his speech is based upon his answers to these questions. Furthermore, he brings the questions down to earth by using a single magazine as a type. Hence the whole speech is supported by a single example, parts of which are examined separately. His overall approach is analytical.

Let me just briefly touch on these questions as they relate to *Digest of Commerce*, but I think maybe I misled you by putting the readers last on the list. You see, like all businesses, our customer is king. We can only continue if our customer knows that he is getting a good value. We at *Digest of Commerce* feel that the way we're best able to cater to our readers is to give importance to his needs, and for this reason, we've studied our reader. We know his average income is about 25,000 dollars. He's a management man in business. He has multiple job responsibilities such as administrative, purchasing, production, personnel, finance, and so forth. We also know of him as a human being. Some lie about their golf scores. As a matter of fact, 1 percent have claimed to have a golf score below the lowest recorded by the PGI. And he takes his wife out for the evening thirty-four times a year. But more importantly, he wants the editorial content of *Digest of Commerce* to satisfy his needs as a management decision-maker. Therefore, every article in *Digest of Commerce* is evaluated by the *Digest of Commerce* editors with a point in view that he does want information that will satisfy these decision-making needs. And this has paid off by the fact that *Digest of Commerce* is considered more management-oriented than any other major publication in our field.

To do this, *Digest of Commerce* has packaged a most unique editorial product. For instance, our outlook sections reporting on business news in a terse telegraphic form pack in so much information that if we were to sell them as a separate service the cost would be about 100 dollars per year. The high cost of developing such a superior editorial product has been borne by advertisers who pay quite a high rate to appear in *Digest of Commerce*. But because the high quality of readers that in many cases appear virtually to study the ads, the cost is truly quite reasonable.

Primarily the advertiser is advertising to communicate to customers and prospects regarding his goods, products, and services, as well as to attract investors. Therefore, he must be assured that he has been reaching the right people with the right message and in a manner that is truly contributing to his goals. To assure that the right people are being reached, several unique efforts have been employed.

Digest of Commerce does not furnish subscriber order blanks. Instead, we have a subscriber application form which we meticulously review prior to acceptance, and as a matter of fact, just last year we turned down 16 thousand applicants because they did not meet our qualifications. By using this method of selectivity, we can offer the advertiser a high concentration of management. About 90 percent of our subscribers have management titles. Every week we do research which shows that advertisements are being read by these management subscribers. These advertising-readership studies show that the ad is read and other research illustrates the effectiveness of the communications.

Using this type of information, we have a sales staff of thirty seasoned salesmen covering the major business firms throughout the country whose job is to document the values of advertising in *Digest of Commerce*. The strongest value is, of course, the purposefulness of the management readers in looking at the editorials and the advertising. So now you can see that this is truly a circle —that the subscriber buys the magazine for the editorial and advertising content and the advertiser buys advertising space to reach the business decision-makers. Unlike some magazines, we cannot determine specifically that our editorial content should be based on previously successful editiorial items. Why? Because we can't determine what the business news will be, and in fact, we consider ourselves to be producing a different product each week.

The order of the points in this speech is determined by the order of the questions; hence the overall organization is clear and effective. There is one exception however. By ostentatiously changing the order and answering the last question first, he gives that point an emphasis which he confirms by treating it at greater length than any other point. Were this change in order inadvertent, it would weaken the speech; as it is, it strengthens it. But this shift also demands a very strong conclusion. The emphasis in the beginning must be repeated at the end, if the audience is to carry away with them the thrust of the speaker's intent.

This speaker supports his answers to the questions with factual information. He demonstrates that a series of questions can be the basis for a successful ordering of thought. There is some variety of evidence provided in the answer to the first question—the golf scores and dinners with wives—but more of this imaginative treatment would strengthen the whole speech. In discussing the final point, the speaker also shows the value of summary, although the summary is more effective if it precedes the point rather than follows it. The summary here leads to the conclusion, but in this instance it would lead more effectively to the final point.

Since this speech was delivered to a group of businessmen, the diction is perhaps appropriate. Almost every human endeavor has its peculiar jargon. Were the speech to be given to a general audience, however, some phrases, such as "decision-making needs," "management-oriented," or "packaged a most unique editorial product," might be changed in order to provide a slightly different tone. In the matter of tone and diction, an audience should be met on its own ground.

The next to last example represents a speech by an expert to a highly informed audience. Speaking to a group of bankers, the vice-president of a large trust company employs description and personal anecdote to support his three points. The general organization describes the functions of two apparently disparate programs, then shows their interaction—a demonstration supported by personal experience.

There are two programs available to exporters of capital-type goods. Both programs are sponsored by the U.S. government. We have the Export-Import Bank program and the FCIA program. The Export-Import Bank program is financing, while the FCIA program is strictly insurance. Under the financing program, which is strictly between the Export-Import Bank and commercial banks, the Export Bank will issue guarantees to commercial banks if the bank will purchase export receivables on a without-recourse basis from a U.S. exporter. Normally the terms run anywhere from three to five years with amortization semiannually. Therefore, if an important client of our bank should ask us to buy a five-year receivable promissory note without recourse, provided we approve the credit of the foreign obligor, we can then approach the Export-Import Bank and ask them to guarantee what we call the latent maturities. These would be the last three-and-one-half years of a five-year transaction. The first year and a half would be for our account and risk without any guarantee at all.

Under the FCIA program the exporter might find that he doesn't need financing; he only wants to get rid of the risks involved in the export sale. You then approach the FCIA asking them to issue you an insurance policy which would protect the exporter from any commercial or political risks that are inherent in the transaction. The FCIA has been criticized by the export community due to the fact that they do not use insurance principles when they consider a specific transaction. It is an insurance association, but too many times it acts like a commercial bank when it examines a specific transaction. The export community per se, therefore, prefers to deal through the commercial banks and the Export-Import Bank. The commercial banks are their traditional lenders, and of course the commercial banks have a vested interest in providing the necessary financing for its clients.

I was asked to sit on the advisory board of FICA. I accepted this appointment because I felt that I could constructively influence some of the decision-making officers of FCIA and the Export-Import Bank of Washington. This is a relatively new advisory group, and it has the normal organizational problems. We have as yet not selected a chairman, although we have been in existence for three months. We have, however, formed what we call an ad hoc committee made up of insurance brokers. Normally, when an exporter looks for FCIA insurance, he doesn't approach the FCIA directly; he goes through his insurance broker. The insurance brokers have many problems. Of course, the main problem is the fact that they feel they do not obtain a sufficient premium, or brokerage. Through the ad hoc committee, the brokers nationally will be able to voice their opinions and comments to the advisory board, and we, of course, hope that we do have ears that will be very receptive to their opinion.

Recently Mr. Linder, who was President of the Export-Import Bank in Washington, made a speech in Florida at the Bankers Association for Foreign Trade convention; at which time he made a startling announcement. He said that the Export-Import Bank was considering opening what he calls a rediscount window at the bank. In a nutshell, this means that commercial banks, if they are financing medium-term exports, will be able to approach the Export-Import Bank and ask the Export-Import Bank to discount the note at a reasonable rate enabling the commercial bank to use those funds for additional export lending. In view of today's trade and balance-of-payments problem, this could be a great asset as far as the promotion of exports from the U.S. is concerned. I would hope that the Export-Import Bank in cooperation with the Federal Reserve Bank and the commercial banks will be able to develop a program that will enable the commercial banks to finance five-year transactions, sell the receivables to the Export-Import Bank with full recourse at a reasonable rate of interest, and thereby enable the commercial banks to use those same funds to provide additional export lending.

This speech is obviously tightly organized and packed with information. The descriptions of the two programs are concise, yet they are supported by brief concrete examples and illustrations. The personal experience adds a great deal of firsthand weight and authority to the speaker's purpose, which is to show the advantages of reciprocal action between the two programs. He further reinforces his point by means of a citation. This is a good instance of a summarized citation, for if Mr. Linder had been quoted at any length, the tempo of the whole speech would be interrupted. For this speech is characterized by a terse, rapidly moving style. A direct quotation would create a lull, which the summary avoids.

It is equally obvious that this is not a speech for a general audience. The speech is studded with terms intelligible only to those whose world is finance. Even the abbreviation FCIA probably would have no meaning for the general public. But certain that both his general concepts and his technical terms are familiar to his audience, the speaker can here cover much ground in a short space of time. He does not have to pause nor to waste a word. Were he addressing a general audience, however, he would have to choose between reducing the number of his points or speaking considerably longer. Such terms as "export receivables," "without-recourse basis," "latent maturities," would require both definition and illustration. Both the tone and the tempo of the speech would then be different. As it is, however, it represents a very good technical speech which has obviously been carefully edited and practiced. In contradistinction to some of the other examples, there are no unconscious repetitions, no vague and inflated phrases.

The final example is offered for your own critical appraisal. This speech was given by an officer of another New York corporation who chose as his topic "The New South." The talk is representative of the efforts of many able, intelligent, informed—but untrained—speakers.

Some of the questions you might ask are the following: Is the simple chronology a sufficient organizing force? How many specific points are there? How is each one developed? Is the speech clear and forceful? If it is, what makes it so? What about diction? How does your latest speech compare to this one?

Most historians stopped its progress economically and industrially from the Civil War, and this is possibly a correct time because up until that point its whole economy was based on an agrarian society. With the end of that war, though, that economy, that culture, that society was completely shattered. Nothing could more vilify what had taken place than the words on the back of an old Confederate note in March of 1865, just prior to the surrender. A Confederate major had written at that point on this note:

"Too poor to preserve the precious ores
Too much of a stranger to borrow.
We issue today our promise to pay
And hope to redeem on the morrow."

The days rolled on and weeks became years, but our coffers were empty. Gold was so scarce that the treasury quaked if a dollar should drop in the till. This situation typified the South at the end of 1865.

The condition prevailed pretty much so until the time of the First World War. There was no Marshall Plan following the Civil War. At no time were there great grants of money. There was little capital to start from. Now, the seedlings began at that point, and it took until the First World War finally to have a government start projects for industrial expansion to finance that war. This was the first infusion of great wealth into the capital structure of the economy. That war only lasted a year and a half. And following that war, it enjoyed in that region of the country the same prosperity the rest of the nation did. But when the industrial slump occurred in the thirties, the South as well as the rest of the nation fell backward and industrial expansion almost ceased which had hardly gotten under way. Having fallen back, it did not begin its progress again until the Second World War.

Thus, you can say that it is only in the past twenty-five years that the real industrial expansion of this region of the country has taken place, and has come into its own, and added strength to the nation. Following the war, it has enjoyed the prosperity that the rest of the nation has enjoyed, and it will continue to do so because it is now creating a base from which capital is being created. And being created, it feeds upon itself to provide more industrial expansion; it has diversified in the fields outside of the agrarian line. Surely the textile mills have moved from New England and are now in the South; the development of the chemical, petrol chemical, all the petroleum fields, all of this is now spreading across the Southland. And I think in the future that you will find that your children will look back upon the agrarian society—that most of us still have fixed in our minds as a thing of the past in history—almost as mythological to us as the Greek civilization is when we read about it.

These examples suggest that there are many ways to develop the body of your speech. The major rules are simple. Your points must be arranged in a clear, coherent, and emphatic order. Each point must be supported, explained, or illustrated in some concrete way.

To achieve these two results, you have a wide variety of means. Your ingenuity, your imagination, and your experience should all come into play as you select the most vivid, colorful, and appropriate means to capture the minds and sympathies of the audience you are to address. The nature of this audience, whether it be large or small, will dictate *how* you develop your ideas as much as *what* ideas you choose to present.

Chapter 7
"AND IN CONCLUSION . . ."

The conclusion of your speech or observations should be satisfying and inevitable. It must fit smoothly and precisely into the structure of your address as a whole. Brief as it ought to be, it is still a vital and complex segment of your remarks. To be successful it must exercise a number of simultaneous functions.

Functions of the Conclusion

First, it is the target at which you have been aiming from the opening words of your speech. In plotting the progress of your address, every point you make and the order in which you arrange those points should be directed toward the conclusion. It is through this process that you make your conclusion inevitable. If any one point checks the flow of thought or seems to divert it, that point should be omitted or placed in a different position. The technique of a detective story in which the ending is held in suspense is not the normal technique for a speech. The audience deserves and expects satisfaction not surprise.

In the second place, the conclusion reminds the audience of the important points you have made. It reminds them or suggests to them the successive states by which your argument is justified. Hopefully this restatement will be couched in fresh words so that the audience will feel that their understanding of your subject is being augmented at the same time that they are reminded of your salient points. Again, the conclusion is the part of your speech which the audience is most likely to carry away with them. For this reason you should polish and revise this part of your speech more than any other. Your choice of words, the compactness and vigor of your style, your rising sense of climax should engage your particular care. Your object is to raise this portion of your speech a little above the rest—no matter how brilliant that may be. A drop in quality or intensity is fatal here, for the manner in which you conclude your speech will make the strongest impression on your audience. Speakers are very much like runners of a mile race—some stagger to the finish line and collapse as they cross it; others finish with a final, stirring burst of speed. Nothing is more painful to hear than a speaker floundering in search of a conclusion. The audience forgets what he had to say and suffers with him or because of him. The difficulty arises because the speaker failed to work out his conclusion in precise detail.

Pace

Pace is an important element in any form of communication. A conversation may be desultory or sparkling; a novel may creep forward or move briskly; a newspaper story may be a tenuous collection of items or a gripping narrative. A steady, brisk movement of thought is a great corrective of dullness. For this reason the pace of your conclusion should never be retarded. Achieving an effective pace does not consist of speaking more rapidly. It is the succession of ideas, not the number of words spoken in a minute, which counts. In your conclusion you should never permit the flow of ideas to slow down or to fall into an eddy. Either of these effects may occur if you try to include too many ideas. The momentum may be lost completely if you attempt a lengthy anecdote or illustration in the course of the conclusion. Supporting material belongs elsewhere. Therefore, this section of your speech requires careful editing if you are to carry a sustained pace to the end.

Restatement

Reminding your audience of the salient points you have made in your speech also takes skill. In the first place, you will be tempted to remind them of too much. Your reminders should be restricted to the major concepts you have advanced. The number will depend upon the length and complexity of your talk, but four or five should be the limit. If these are formed into a strong, logical chain, you can trust your audience to recall both the lesser propositions and the supporting material. You must remember that you are reminding your audience, not offering a second version of your speech. It is important that you try to find fresh terms in which to clothe these reminders. Putting your thought into slightly different words will reinforce as well as recall the impact your original version had upon the audience. Since different terms produce different effects upon those who hear them, the audience may well feel that in the conclusion they have been provided with a new insight rather than a simple reminder.

Because the conclusion is the final impression you make, that impression should reveal you as a warm, vital, poised, and logical speaker. The conclusion must rise rather than diminish in intensity. It should leave the audience satisfied, yet eager for more. Such an effect demands careful wording so that the conclusion is tighter, more compressed, than the relatively expansive middle part of the speech. The burden of proof or of persuasion—with its accompanying evidence, illustration, and argument—is the function of the middle part; the function of the conclusion is summation. Hence the order of thought must be such that an increasing significance and an increasing pace will lead to the final words. Here both judgment and restraint are all important. You should devote extra time to polishing and editing this segment of any talk.

As a speaker you may be tempted to let your well-supported and well-documented material plead its own case. In theory it should be strong enough to do so and to make the conclusion a mere formality. But in practice not all the audience will be alert to the full implications of your discourse. These implications should be vigorously reasserted in your conclusion. Because they represent your attitude toward the material you have discussed, that attitude must be reflected in your final words. Hence a conclusion which gives the impression of being perfunctory also gives the impression of a speaker who lacks the conviction and vigor to provide complete support for his thesis. Whatever tone and attitude you have adopted through the body of your speech should be intensified as you move through the conclusion. When you rise to the climax, you must carry your audience with you.

Your Purpose Accomplished

From a second point of view, the conclusion is just as important. One of the major controlling factors in your speech is purpose. That purpose was mentioned, or at least implied, in your introduction. Hopefully it was justified and established in the central part of the speech. In the conclusion that purpose should be validated in a clear and positive manner. You should be able to make a statement which your audience will accept on the basis of what you have presented to them—its logic, evidence, and persuasiveness. Expressions such as "I have attempted to show . . ." or "My purpose in this talk has been to . . ." are confessions of failure. They suggest that you are conscious that your purpose is too obscure to be understood unless you explain it or that your audience is too obtuse to grasp it. Neither alternative belongs in your conclusion. Actually the conclusion is similar to the end of a geometric proof: "Therefore the two triangles are congruent." Your conclusion should be based on a strict logical chain in which no vital link has been neglected. The QED which follows the geometric proof is a reminder to you that your purpose can be clearly validated and firmly stated only if your demonstration has proceeded from one logical step to the next. So the conclusion furnishes a convenient review for you as a speaker. You should ask yourself whether your purpose is resolved and justified by what you have actually said. Sometimes there is a significant difference between intent and actual performance. You may be claiming credit for steps which you assumed, but did not actually take. As you looked ahead to your conclusion when you composed your introduction, so you should look back to your introduction from the conclusion. Does your conclusion fulfill all the expectations you aroused in the opening of your speech?

The Final Words

The final words of the conclusion carry a special weight. Many speeches are remembered for the ringing words which ended them. Excellent conclusions are more often spoiled by the addition of an unnecessary sentence or two than by any other fault. An audience is sensitive to anticlimax. Provide the best concluding sentence you can compose, and let nothing persuade you to say an additional word when you have uttered it. Even in a purely impromptu speech, you should be quick to recognize when you have hit upon a firm ending and stop right there. Indeed in making an impromptu speech, your first thought should be for your concluding sentence. Otherwise you have no target toward which to direct your thought.

A Variety of Examples

The principles of restatement, careful wording, compactness of thought, and rising intensity can be illustrated through the final words of three well-known speeches from the past century. Granted that the style has changed, the principles have not. The first example is the conclusion of a speech in support of the reform bill delivered in Parliament by Thomas Babington Macaulay in 1831.

> The danger is terrible. The time is short. If this bill should be rejected, I pray to God that none of those who concur in rejecting it may ever remember their votes with unavailing remorse amidst the wreck of laws, the confusion of ranks, the spoilation of property, and the dissolution of social order.

Here the sense of urgency is established in two short, emphatic sentences. Earnestness of tone is conveyed by the appeal to the deity. Then the audience is reminded of the thrust of the speaker's argument that rejection of the bill would be fatal to law, government, order, property, and society. Here is the gist of his speech in vigorous, rapid and emotional language.

The second example exhibits an entirely different tone with even greater earnestness. It is not a trumpet call; it is organ music. But it, too, rises to a climax in which all that was said before is summarized and pulled together. It is the conclusion of Lincoln's second inaugural address given in 1865.

> With malice toward none, with charity for all, with firmness in the right, as God gives us to see the right, let us strive on to finish the work we are now in, to bind up the nation's wounds, to care for him who shall have borne the battle, and for his widow and orphans; to do all that may cherish a just and lasting peace among ourselves and with all nations.

Were it not for the fact that Lincoln was a master of words, this conclusion would be impossible to speak. It is all one sentence. Lincoln has overcome that difficulty by providing frequent natural pauses in his strongly rhythmical prose. A modern speaker would use shorter sentences. But as he reviews the topics of his speech, Lincoln rises to a magnificent climax by lifting the concept of peace from the individual, to the nation, and finally to the world. No additional phrase could do anything but spoil the effect.

The third example in chronological order is William Jennings Bryan's "cross of gold" speech at the Democratic Convention in 1896. This is the conclusion of that speech.

> Having behind us the productive masses of this nation and the world, supported by the commercial interests, the laboring interests, and the toilers everywhere, we

will answer their demand for a gold standard by saying to them: You shall not press down upon the brow of mankind this crown of thorns; you shall not crucify mankind upon a cross of gold.

This is an excellent example of a speech which is remembered chiefly for its conclusion and is included here to illustrate the point. It rises to an emotional intensity which is not common today, but the rise is impressive. The intensity could take another form in a present-day speech, but it must be *present*. Like the other examples, this one contains a summary of the points which have been covered in the body of the speech. Bryan's purpose is made plainly evident. It is presented as a metaphor rather than as flat statement. That the metaphor involves a comparison between Bryan's convictions and the religious beliefs of many of his hearers gives it compelling and dramatic weight.

Finally, here are three conclusions recorded on tape. Again, you should bear in mind that these are taken from short addresses prepared for speech classes. They were not read from a manuscript. They do indicate that good intentions do not always achieve happy results.

The first comes from a talk on the function of a supervisor. Given by the vice-president of a corporation, the speech had for its thesis the need for effective communication. This is the conclusion.

> In closing, I would like to leave you with an illustration that I think best describes this whole talk. And that is—there are really three kinds of employees or workers in an organization. The first group is a group who makes

things happen . . . the people who generate action,
and we might call this the definition for a supervisor or
manager. The second group is the one who sits aside on
the sidelines. They are very aware that action is taking
place, and they are able to bend with it and fulfill a
project or a job. And the third is that group, if you will,
who sits on the sidelines, doesn't know anything is hap-
pening and really they probably never will. The point is,
in which group are you going to be?

Here the speaker had to identify his conclusion by
saying, "In closing." Actually that identification is necessary here, because his final remarks do not touch upon
his thesis—effective communication. His purpose, therefore, is neglected. He announces his intention of presenting a summarizing illustration, but provides a statement
instead. The statement does touch upon a classification
he had made earlier, but it is too long, too wordy, and
too inconclusive. In the end, he throws the resolution of
his thought back to the audience. Careful editing and a
glance backward to his purpose and thesis might have
rescued this conclusion. Had he edited this important
section of his speech, the third sentence would probably
read: "The first group—supervisors or managers—make
things happen; they generate action." The rest of the
passage also should be made more compact and forceful.

The second example comes from a talk on the relative
safety of private flying. It was given by an investment
counselor, who concluded as follows:

My point at this time is that in 1949 automobiles
killed about 12 per cent less people per mile driven than
they do today, while aircraft progressed to two times

their safety record. With the development of electronics and the phasing out of the older, less-forgiving aircraft, we find the safety record is constantly improving, and I would like to forecast that in fifteen years, flying your own aircraft will be as safe as driving your own automobile to the grocery store.

Here the speaker has found a substitute expression for "in conclusion" but the effect is the same. If the point is well made, the speaker does not have to identify it. Here, too, the conclusion might have been effective if the final words had been carefully thought out. As it is, the wording is cloudy and inexact. The final statement would be much stronger had it read: "In fifteen years flying your own aircraft will be as safe as driving your automobile to the grocery store." In this conclusion, however, the author does return to his thesis, and he does express his purpose. The effect is vitiated by lack of attention to precise and vigorous wording. The contrast in the opening sentence of the segment is not made vivid enough, for instance.

The final example is an effective conclusion of a short talk. The speaker was an editor in a publishing house whose purpose was to explain the advantages of teaching a child to type. You will remember that the first part of this talk served as one example of a beginning. Subsequently he had developed several points by means of statistics, psychological studies, and experiment. In a very brief conclusion, he hammered home both his purpose and his thesis. He made most effective use of a rising intensity through the repetition of a key phrase. In actual delivery it is easy to put a greater stress on the phrase each time it is spoken. In contrast to the two previous examples, this conclusion could have nothing added to it. It is a strong ending.

> Teach your child to type so he will surpass his classmates in words, spelling, and reading. Teach your child to type so he gains a skill that will cut his writing time to one-third, all the rest of his life. *Teach your child to type!*

Your conclusion is probably the most important section of your speech. It deserves your most careful attention. It should be short, strongly and economically worded, concentrated in thought. In it you should summarize your chief points, reaffirm your purpose, and validate your thesis. While the whole conclusion should be as carefully worded as your talent will allow, the final sentence must be worked over with special care. The tempo of your thought should rise strongly enough to carry your audience with you to the very last phrase. It is through a moving and effective conclusion that you reap your reward as a speaker—the warm and instant response of a pleased audience.

Chapter 8
THE WHOLE AS THE SUM OF ITS PARTS

Since you have examined portions of speeches given by editors, bankers, and officers of corporations, it seems appropriate to provide an example of a complete speech. It might be a good idea, also, to examine an address delivered by a practiced and skillful speaker. But a speech long enough to display the full power of the speaker and to exemplify most of the points you have considered would occupy a disproportionate space. Hence the example which follows is only part of a much longer address. Nevertheless the part is so well organized that it can serve as surrogate for a much longer speech. Furthermore, had time been a factor for the speaker, it might have stood by itself as an effective brief address.

Short as it is, the excerpt supports many of the principles advocated in the chapters which deal with the beginning, the development, and the ending of a speech. It suggests that these principles must be employed with the speech as a whole constantly in your mind. The tone, the attitude, the diction, the point of view in each part of the speech must be brought into harmony so that there is a smooth flow of thought from beginning to end. The transitions between parts must be as clear and cohesive as the transitions within the sections. The segment which stands here for the whole speech illustrates a carefully planned, organized, and coherent exposition by a craftsman in the art of speaking.

The Tone or Attitude

Thomas H. Huxley delivered this address to a group of English workingmen in 1863. It is well to remember that Huxley was one of the most distinguished scholars, as well as the most articulate scientist, of his age—an age in which science was the most controversial of subjects. Unlike the present, when scientists speak with an almost divine authority, the scientist was then likely to face a hostile audience rather than an awed one. At that time the apparent conflict between science and religion had made scientists objects of denunciation and suspicion. So an audience of workingmen was more likely to be influenced by the pulpit than by the professor's chair. Moreover, the gulf between a learned scholar like Huxley and an audience of workingmen was far wider then than the gap in understanding between a scientist and a group of factory workers now. So Huxley had a very difficult problem of communication across the gulf which separated his powerful, highly trained mind from the minds of men for whom science was a mystery. Huxley's success or failure in this difficult undertaking—a success or failure which you will have to judge—strikes at the heart of the problem of oral communication.

The Introduction

His title did not help Huxley much. In the style of the day, it read, "The Method by Which the Causes of the Present and Past Conditions of Organic Nature Are to Be Discovered." Such a title is enough to paralyze any audience, and today it would be intolerable. Yet once into his address, Huxley immediately reassures his audience. He at once provides the *spark*, namely, the challenge to understand the methods of science to persons who are ignorant both of science and of its methodology. A challenge is always a stimulus, particularly if the audience is assured that they are capable of meeting it. And Huxley insists that they are capable. There is really a double challenge here—first, to the intellect and, second, to the imagination, for a mystery dares the imagination and the explication of the mystery produces a satisfaction over and above the intellectual triumph gained by understanding new material. Huxley also expresses his *purpose* in his opening words; i.e., to show that the method of scientific investigation "is nothing but the expression of the necessary mode of working of the human mind."

He proposes, then, to enkindle the *spark* by showing that the mystery of scientific method can be explained in terms of the natural operation of man's mind and that intellectually the audience is entirely capable of understanding that operation. The *purpose* is at once supported by a brief analogy which successfully meets the problem at two levels—the baker or butcher contrasted to the chemist, and the common scales contrasted to the balance and finely graduated weights. The contrast in diction between *scales* and *balance* heightens the effect.

But before there is any further comment on technique, you might read the selection itself.

> The method of scientific investigation is nothing but the expression of the necessary mode of working of the human mind. It is simply the mode at which all phenomena are reasoned about, rendered precise and exact. There is no more difference, but there is just the same kind of difference, between the mental operations of a man of science and those of an ordinary person, as there is between the operations and methods of a baker or of a butcher weighing out his goods in common scales and the operations of a chemist in performing a difficult and complex analysis by means of his balance and finely graduated weights. It is not that the action of the scales in the one case and the balance in the other differ in the principles of their construction or manner of working; but the beam of one is set on an infinitely finer axis than the other and of course, turns by the addition of a much smaller weight.
>
> You will understand this better, perhaps, if I give you some familiar example. You have all heard it repeated, I dare say, that men of science work by means of induction and deduction, and that by the help of these operations they, in a sort of sense, wring from nature certain other things which are called natural laws and causes, and that out of these, by some cunning skill of their

own, they build up hypotheses and theories. And it is imagined by many that the operations of the common mind can be by no means compared with these processes, and that they have to be acquired by a sort of special apprenticeship to the craft. To hear all these large words, you would think that the mind of a man of science must be constituted differently from that of his fellow men; but if you will not be frightened by terms, you will discover that you are quite wrong and that all these terrible apparatus are being used by yourselves every day and every hour of your lives.

There is a well-known incident in one of Molière's plays where the author makes the hero express unbounded delight on being told that he had been talking prose during the whole of his life. In the same way, I trust that you will take comfort and be delighted with yourselves on the discovery that you have been acting on the principles of inductive and deductive philosophy during the same period. Probably there is not one here who has not in the course of the day had occasion to set in motion a complex train of reasoning of the very same kind, though differing, of course, in degree, as that which a scientific man goes through in tracing the causes of natural phenomena.

A very trivial circumstance will serve to exemplify this. Suppose you go into a fruiterer's shop, wanting an apple. You take up one, and on biting it you find it is sour; you look at it and see that it is hard and green. You take up another one, and that too is hard, green and sour. The shopman offers you a third; but before biting it you examine it and find that it is also hard and green; and you immediately say that you will not have it, as it must be sour like those you have already tried.

Nothing can be more simple than that, you think; but if you will take the trouble to analyze and trace out into its logical elements what has been done by the mind, you will be greatly surprised. In the first place you have performed the operation of induction. You found that in two experiences hardness and greenness in apples go together with sourness. It was so in the first case, and it was confirmed by the second. True, it is a very small basis, but still it is enough to make an induction from; you generalize the facts, and you expect to find sourness in apples where you get hardness and greenness. You found upon that a general law that all hard and green apples are sour; and that, so far as it goes, is a perfect induction.

Well, having got your natural law in this way, when you are offered another apple which you find is hard and green, you say, " 'All hard and green apples are sour; this apple is hard and green, therefore this apple is sour.' " That train of reasoning is what logicians call a syllogism and has all its various parts and terms—its major premise, its minor premise, and its conclusion. And by the help of further reasoning, which if drawn out would have to be exhibited in two or three other syllogisms, you arrive at your final determination, "I will not have that apple." So that, you see, you have in the first place, established a law by induction, and upon that you have founded a deduction and reasoned out the special conclusion of the particular case.

Well now, suppose, having got your law, that at some time afterwards you are discussing the qualities of apples with a friend. You will say to him, " 'It is a very curious thing, but I find that all hard and green apples are sour!' " Your friend says to you, " 'But how do you know

that?' " You at once reply, " 'Oh, because I have tried
them over and over again and have always found them
to be so.' " Well, if we were talking science instead of
common sense, we should call this an experimental verification. And if still opposed to go further and say, " 'I
have heard from people in Somersetshire and Devon-
shire, where a large number of apples are grown, that
they have observed the same thing. It is also found to be
the case in Normandy and in North America. In short, I
find it to be the universal experience of mankind
wherever attention has been directed to the subject.' "
Whereupon your friend, unless he is a very unreason-
able man, agrees with you and is convinced that you are
quite right in the conclusion you have drawn. He believes, although perhaps he does not know he believes it,
the more extensive verifications are, the more frequently
experiments have been made and results of the same
kind arrived at, the more varied the conditions under
which the same results have been attained, the more
certain is the ultimate conclusion. And he disputes the
question no further. He sees that the experiment has
been tried under all sorts of conditions as to time, place,
and people with the same result; and he says to you,
therefore, that the law you have laid down must be a
good one and he must believe it.

In science we do the same thing; the philosopher
exercises precisely the same faculties, though in a much
more delicate manner. In scientific inquiry it becomes a
matter of duty to expose a supposed law to every possible kind of verification, and to take care, moreover,
that this is done intentionally and not left to mere accident as in the case of the apples. And in science, as in
common life, our confidence in a law is in exact propor-

tion to the absence of verifications. For instance, if you let go your grasp of an article you may have in your hand, it will immediately fall to the ground. That is a very common verification of one of the best established laws of nature, that of gravitation.

The method by which men of science established the existence of that law is exactly the same as that by which we have established the trivial proposition about the sourness of hard and green apples. But we believe it in such an extensive, thorough, and unhesitating manner because the universal experience of mankind verifies it, and we can verify it ourselves at any time; and that is the strongest possible foundation on which any natural law can rest.

So much by way of proof that the method of establishing laws in science is exactly the same as that pursued in common life.

Huxley has recognized his first duty as a speaker—to weigh and estimate his audience. Because he is speaking to workingmen, he adopts a simple and direct manner. Yet it is at once apparent that he is not talking down to them. There is no trace of a superior or patronizing air. Instead he injects warmth and ease by speaking to them directly as "you." Were you to read another speech by Huxley, one in which he addresses a group of fellow scientists, you would find an entirely different tone. Yet even a sophisticated audience could not take offense at the *tone* of this speech. The audience is treated with dignity and ease; they are encouraged and subtly praised. The only concession to them comes from the nature of the examples and analogies. They are simple and familiar; yet they would be equally effective with a more learned group.

The Organization

The *organization* of the speech depends upon the definition and explanation of certain abstract philosophical and scientific terms. Having promised that he will provide a familiar example—once again reassuring his audience—Huxley introduces such terms as *induction, deduction, hypothesis* and *theory*. Then he once more calms the apprehensions of his audience by informing them that it is the terms, not the processes, which are unfamiliar to them. At this point he also injects a touch of humor by quoting Molière. The *quotation* does more than add humor; it flatters the audience by assuming that they know who Molière is and that they can catch the point. But in employing the quotation he is also tactful. A speaker thinking of himself rather than of his audience would show off his superior attainments by quoting Molière in French. But with delicate consideration for his audience, Huxley quotes the dramatist indirectly rather than directly. He gives the substance of Molière's remarks—not the actual words.

The Method of Development

In developing his thought, therefore, Huxley uses a number of methods. He tends to combine these methods rather than to bring them in one by one, yet you will at once see that he depends upon *definition, quotation, analogy,* and *example.* It is interesting to observe his use of analogy to support definition. The fact that the analogy is drawn from a homely and common experience enhances rather than detracts from its effectiveness. It meets another test for a good analogy: It serves to explain and illustrate his thesis at a number of points. Huxley shows that experience with hard green apples enables one to develop a hypothesis through the inductive process. The same analogy shows the hypothesis applied to the selection of a single apple through the deductive process. Moreover, the analogy helps to define scientific verification and hence the process by which an hypothesis becomes a theory. In the course of his remarks he is able to define and explain a syllogism—a term which well might have repelled his audience if he had not brought it in to the current of his thought in a natural and disarming way.

As an experienced and confident speaker, Huxley introduces dialogue to enliven and make more dramatic a rather austere topic. Effective as this technique may be in this instance, you should employ it with caution. Dialogue either succeeds brilliantly or fails miserably; it seldom falls into middle ground. Natural, easy dialogue can be most effective, but it is difficult to compose. If you attempt it, be sure that someone whose critical taste you trust passes judgment on it. Observe, too, that Huxley places the dialogue just at the point where the audience needs some relief or stimulus. The closely drawn analogy had demanded the concentrated attention of the audience up to that point. Another speaker might have injected a touch of humor or a very brief anecdote at that time to provide the same effect. The brief relaxation offered to the audience permits Huxley to make his final point—the importance of scientific verification—in a strong, straightforward way. He does not need further example, illustration, or analogy.

The Conclusion

As he draws to a conclusion, you will observe that Huxley employs the principle of *restatement*. In the sixth paragraph he pulls his thought together. He reminds his audience of the progress which he and they have made together. Part of the restatement is fairly explicit, but much of it is implicit. Once again he flatters and compliments his audience by assuming that, in Polonius' words, they can "by indirection find direction out." Yet he keeps a discreet control of their imaginations by providing a brief and simple analogy which confirms and parallels the long analogy he had used previously. Again in this summary he puts particular emphasis on his main point—that scientific law depends upon the universal experience of mankind.

If you have difficulty with your actual conclusions, you might weigh the effect of Huxley's single, incisive sentence. It is true that this sentence is to lead to the next major division of his speech; yet for the segment, it is a firm declaration that his purpose has been achieved. Since his purpose was established at the very beginning of the speech, this conclusion rounds off the address and makes it a carefully organized whole. It is like the QED of a geometric proof.

Transitions

As you look at this whole, you might observe Huxley's transitions. They are simple ones because he did not wish to place too great a burden on his audience. The movement from the introduction to the presentation of terms, from the terms to the long analogy, and from the analogy to the principle of scientific verification is accomplished by a direct reference in the first sentence of each section to a word or a thought in the last sentence of the preceding section. Because he wishes to be plain, Huxley uses a simple *this* or *that*. However, the transition between the second and third paragraphs is a little more subtle. It is effected by repeating an idea in different words. The "every day and every hour of your lives" in the second paragraph becomes "during the whole of his life" in the third. It is the careful attention to these transitions which is responsible for the smooth and rapid flow of thought. The transitions are an argument for the importance of detail in making your speech as a whole effective.

This excerpt reveals preparation and organization on Huxley's part. His tone and his approach are governed by the audience he is addressing. He is careful to define abstract and technical terms and to develop his definitions through example, analogy, and quotation. His points are arranged in order of importance. He devotes more space to his final point and places greater emphasis on it than on any other single point. In addition to ensuring that his address has unity, he has seen to it that by careful attention to transitions his remarks are coherent. In a brief and trenchant statement, his conclusion sums up his purpose. Here you have a useful model of the common expository speech.

Chapter 9

PRACTICE MAKES PERFECT

Once you have organized your speech and have developed and worded the three component parts, then you must practice it. Whether you propose to speak from a manuscript or from a series of notes, you still must practice if you are to produce a polished effort. The art of the speaker and the art of the actor are not so far apart that one can neglect the careful rehearsal that is so necessary for the other. A speaker cannot project himself outward toward his audience when his attention is directed inward in a struggle to keep track of his order of thought or his wording. Nor can he exercise control over his audience when his eyes are glued to his script. He must be so much a master of his words and material that he can devote his full attention to his audience. He can hardly expect the concentrated attention of the audience when his is directed primarily to his notes or his script. Therefore, you must practice.

The amount of practice, however, will vary according to the experience of the speaker and to the importance of the occasion. Even a veteran speaker should rehearse his speech—but he will not depend upon rehearsal to build his confidence as will a relatively inexperienced speaker—for there are always problems of pace and timing which can be resolved only by practicing the speech with a critical eye on your own performance. Beyond these problems, however, the inexperienced speaker must establish a pattern which is so firm that no minor incident while on the platform will disturb his equanimity. After all, the electronic equipment may misbehave or people in the audience faint or create a disturbance, but the well-rehearsed speaker can pick up his speech after the hiatus without being seriously disconcerted. The other factor, the importance of the occasion, depends upon common sense. A busy pediatrician speaking to the PTA will pay his audience the courtesy of preparing his remarks with care and of speaking as well as he can. On the other hand, the time he can devote to rehearsal will be limited by the press of his duties. But if he is to address a convention of the American Medical Association on a special phase of pediatrics, the occasion is so vital to his professional reputation that he must practice until his address is as effective as he can make it.

Speaking from Notes

The type of practice will depend somewhat on the method you propose to use. If you are reading from a script, then part of the rehearsal should be devoted to the principles and suggestions contained later in this chapter. But if you are simply using notes, your practice will take on a different emphasis. In speaking from notes, the order of your thought is indicated, but these thoughts are not put into words. Hence your rehearsal will concentrate on establishing key words or phrases which will ensure the smooth flow of your discourse and will forestall awkward pauses as you grope for the precise term. Ideally, the notes should not be necessary, although they are often a source of assurance to a speaker. But if they are used as a substitute for careful rehearsal, they can become a dangerous trap. Unless you have practiced carefully, you may give too much or too little time to a specific point. In that situation you may have to slight one or more subsequent points, or worse, you may sense that you are reaching your conclusion too quickly. Then you will be tempted to pad or inflate your final point or two—and so blunt their impact. It is only careful rehearsal against a clock that will bring into harmony the balance and proportion of your speech and the time at your disposal.

The time-honored device of practicing before a mirror is artificial for two reasons. First, you see yourself at very close range. The audience, seeing you at a greater distance, may not share the effect you are attempting to produce. Second, and more important, as Aristotle remarked—people are poor judges of their own causes. The expression which seems to you to indicate firmness and decision may seem to the audience an indication of a gestative disturbance. When you fancy you are being earnest, you may appear to others dour and forbidding. What you consider a winning smile—especially if you turn it off and on—may seem to the audience to be a nervous tic. Or it may resemble the artificial grin which so often results when a photographer urges his sitter to smile or "look pleasant." A mirror is not necessarily an accurate reporter.

In most situations, practicing before a mirror is not practical. True, your attention is drawn to your appearance as you deliver the speech. But your attention is likely to be so drawn to appearance that you fail to concentrate on what you are saying and how you are saying it. You are apt to scant considerations of timing, emphasis, and inflection. You may slight the variations in pace and the significant pauses which provide much of the color in an effective speech. Of course, if practicing before a mirror gives you confidence, you should continue to rehearse in that fashion, but there are better ways to prepare yourself.

Listening to Yourself with a Critical Ear

The first of these methods is to record your speech on a tape recorder. Then with the aid of pencil and paper you can make a critical appraisal of your effort. Here you must be as objective as possible; you must put yourself in the position of a member of your audience. You will ask yourself whether, from the point of view of the audience, the material you are presenting is clear, convincing, well ordered; whether the points you make are adequately supported; whether the transitions preserve a logical flow of thought; and whether the conclusion is a strong affirmation of your purpose. Have you included material which is not directly relevant to the issue you are discussing? Furthermore, you can check grammar, pronunciation, diction, and inflection. The tape recording should also be timed, because one of its prime advantages is that it provides you with an accurate measure of the ratio between what you want to say and the time at your disposal. After the first taping you may have to make substantial revisions in order to conform to your allotted time. The answer to excessive material is not an increase in pace of delivery, if the pace of the rehearsal is satisfactory. A careful study of the notes you have taken should prepare you for a second session with the tape recorder.

At this point you should remind yourself that there is a difference between written and oral communication. Material which appears to be effective in manuscript, or which follows a logical sequence as it appears in notes, may not sound so smooth and emphatic when it is spoken. The diction of the written word may involve you in combinations of sound which are difficult to articulate clearly. Listening to the tape, you may find that you have unconsciously repeated words too frequently, or that you have tended to use too many abstract or polysyllabic words. You may find that certain words are stumbling blocks for you and as such should be avoided. You may even find that a shift or two in the order of your presentation will enable you to speak more easily and more convincingly.

If you are speaking from notes and if you wish to take

particular pains with the speech, you might have the tape transcribed. Seeing it in typescript may reveal wordy, repetitious, or awkward passages. The examples cited in the chapter dealing with the parts of a speech suggest the value of transcription. Had these able and intelligent speakers seen their remarks reduced to type, they would certainly have made changes in wording, order, or emphasis. Transcription provides one more check that your intent and your performance coincide.

With the revisions and emendations complete, you are ready for a second session with the tape recorder. This second rehearsal should prove to be more rewarding than the first one because most of the flaws evident in the first recording will be eliminated. So this recording can emphasize pace and timing. However, if the revisions have been drastic, you may be so concentrating on changes in order or in diction that you are more concerned with detail than with overall effect. In that case you may wish to rehearse the speech on tape a third time to gain control over the tempo of the whole speech. Although it is difficult to speak with verve and animation in the absence of a live audience, these repetitions will give you such confidence that you will be able to speak with only casual references to your script or notes.

Reducing the Speech to a Summary or Digest

Another very effective way of practicing your speech is to give a digest of it. From antiquity to the present time, the précis has been a most useful tool in ordering thought and in making every word count. Although he was speaking of epic or tragedy, Aristotle's words apply as cogently to speeches.[1]

> His story, again, whether already made or of his own making, he should first simplify and reduce to a universal form, before proceeding to lengthen it out by the insertion of episodes.

He illustrates the method by so reducing the *Odyssey*.

> A certain man has been abroad many years; Poseidon is ever on the watch for him, and he is all alone. Matters at home too have come to this, that his substance has been wasted and his son's death plotted by suitors to his wife. Then he arrives there himself after his grievous sufferings; reveals himself, and falls on his enemies; and the end is his salvation and their death. This being all that is proper to the *Odyssey*, everything else in it is episode.

If *illustration* is substituted for *episode*, Aristotle's words apply to the summary of a speech. His words are carefully chosen so that each one contains the essence of an idea which is expanded in the full account and so that hardly a word could be omitted. As you discuss your speech with your wife or with close friends, a similar précis will fix the outline firmly in your mind. It will help you to select key words, and it will bolster your confidence. You must simply be sure that the précis contains the essence of your opening, your purpose, your example or examples, and your conclusion. Just as a black-and-white sketch of a painting arouses a desire in

[1] Richard McKeon, *Introduction to Aristotle*, Modern Library, Inc., New York.

the viewer to see the original; so your précis should make your wife or friends eager for the full speech. They should look forward to the color, the detail, the shadings, the tones, which are necessarily missing in the sketch. If they approve the précis, you may conclude, *a fortiori*, that they will approve the whole address. So your confidence is further strengthened.

Combining Sight with Sound

The third, and most effective, way to practice your speech is to record it on video tape or sound film. This method should probably be preceded by one or two sessions with the tape recorder to eliminate most of the obviously rough spots. Most large corporations now have apparatus for recording on video tape, but it is also readily available for those who wish to rent it. This method of rehearsal is particularly important for those who have to deliver important speeches or who must speak before a large audience. It should be almost mandatory for anyone who is to speak on television. A mirror essentially reveals how you appear to yourself. A video tape or a sound film as it appears on a screen is sufficiently distant from you so that you really see how you appear to others. Furthermore your voice, apparently issuing from your image on the screen, will have an effect somewhat different from that of your voice recorded on tape. The combination of sight and sound will give you an objective view of yourself which is unrivaled. No other medium will reveal to you quite so accurately how your personality affects others. Many speakers, viewing themselves on video tape or sound film for the first time, have been shocked to discover how different the image and voice on the screen was from the image and voice they thought they were projecting. As a result they have made changes which produced dramatic improvement. These media also permit you to check on the stiffness or ease of your posture, the grace or awkwardness of your gestures, and the presence of nervous mannerisms you may have thought you had overcome. If your speech is important, or if such equipment is easily available, you should consider one or more rehearsals with video tape or sound film.

Speaking from a Manuscript

Here a word should be said about practicing a speech which you propose to read from a manuscript. Your object in practicing is to develop a technique which gives the audience the impression that you are not reading at all—that you are speaking almost extemporaneously. The first step toward creating that impression is to become thoroughly familiar with your text. Being familiar with the text does not mean memorizing it word for word, however. You can hardly concentrate on an easy, responsive attitude toward your audience and on a considerable feat of memory at the same time. Memorization may make you stiff and stilted as you strive to let not a syllable of your text escape you. Rather you should have in mind the form of your introduction, the number and order of your points, the illustrations for each one, your transitions, and in more detail, the wording of your conclusion. Then you should turn to the tape recorder. Having practiced reading and recording several times to check your tempo, your emphasis, your shifts in tone or volume—all of which are important to good reading or speaking—record the speech without using your text. This process will have two effects. You will discover that actually you do not have to rely heavily on your text. You will also find places that may give you some difficulty. These you can mark on your manuscript for special attention. Your typescript then becomes an aid upon which you lean lightly as you devote your attention to the audience.

The free rendition of your speech should be practiced more than once. It will prove to be a guide to tempo and tone, for people tend to read faster and more woodenly than they speak. If the speech is an important one, you might finish with a session on video tape. Through this you can learn whether your head follows your eyes to the script so that you are speaking to the lectern rather than to the audience. If you do drop your head, you lose eye contact and also tend to become inaudible. You can also learn whether your practice sessions have made you so independent of your text that your contact with the audience will be direct and compelling. The more you are freed from a word-by-word dependence on your script, the more ease and confidence you will have, the more shading and interpretation you can give to your words. Your text, then, becomes a gentle guide to steady you, to remind you of difficult places, but not to carry you on its back.

Practice with tape allows you to sit in judgment on

your own performance. It permits you to go through the whole speech and only then to look for weaknesses. If you practice by asking your wife or a friend to comment on your speech, your critic will have to interrupt the flow of your thought and expression or else trust to memory to recall portions that need further attention. However, if you can adopt a critical and detached view of your own performance, you will be the best judge as to whether the recorded speech fulfills your intent. If the recorded speech does meet with your approval—if you follow your manuscript spontaneously—the live speech will be even more satisfactory.

You owe your audience the best effort of which you are capable. Yet failure to rehearse your speech may spoil in its delivery a discourse which you have taken infinite pains to prepare, organize, and develop. Much has been said about practice as a means of developing confidence —for so it does—but practice also polishes and refines a speech, gives it sparkle and vigor. Hence the overconfident speaker can err by neglecting sufficient rehearsal and by so doing not gain the perfection which his audience deserves. It is well to remember that all your preparation leads to those moments when you stand before your audience. You must be ready for them.

Chapter 10
A FEW WELL-CHOSEN WORDS

In speaking of the various forms of art, Aristotle insisted that they were imitations of nature and that they differed in their means, their objects, and their manner. From that point of view, the art of oral communication has for its means *words*. This is man's oldest and most important art. Without it there could have been no civilization, yet at the present time, it is not practiced as an art to the degree that it was practiced in classical antiquity. That was an age in which almost all history, science, politics, and literature were transmitted by word of mouth. Advancement in law, in government, in learning, in the military life depended on the art of speaking. Even during the Middle Ages, the art of public discourse retained its primacy. Although for a time the printing press put oral communication in a secondary place as an art to be cultivated, radio, television, and the increasing complexity of organized society seem to be restoring a balance between the art of speaking and the art of writing. For although words are the means for both arts, they are not used in quite the same way in each art. The manner is different.

Words as Audible Symbols

Words are, after all, merely symbols for ideas. Some of the symbols are infinitely complex. The word *man*, for instance, can represent the concept of humanity in general, of intellect as opposed to nonintellect, of limited power as opposed to omnipotence, of an individual person, of the masculine as opposed to the feminine—to mention a very few. *Television*, on the other hand, is an arbitrary, invented word which symbolizes a much narrower concept. Since most people cannot think except through the medium of these symbols, the quality of their thought depends directly on the precision and the extent of their vocabulary. In a series of studies published a few years ago, Mr. Johnson O'Connor of the Stevens Institute made a strong case for the direct relationship between an extensive vocabulary and success in life—no matter what business or profession a man pursued. By its very nature, too, English is a language with an enormous vocabulary, one which easily admits new words or words borrowed from other languages. Therefore, when you speak in English, you have great resources to draw upon.

Of course words are not the only symbols for communication. Mathematics, physics, chemistry, all are sciences with symbols of their own for immediate and precise communicative ideas. Music, pantomime, the dance convey ideas through sound or movement. These ideas may be of great importance, but they are intelligible only to those who are specially trained to receive them. As Aristotle would say, the *means* of communication are different. But even when words are used, a difference exists when it is the ear rather than the eye which receives the symbols. The eye can move at any speed it wishes; the ear must adjust to the speed of the speaker. As long as the eye recognizes the word, correct pronunciation is a matter of indifference—not so when the word is spoken. When the idea is complex or difficult, the eye can run through the words again in a second effort to understand. The auditor has a single chance to catch the speaker's meaning. On the other hand, tone of voice, inflection, emphasis, timing, can give a richness and significance to the spoken word which only the most skilled reader can supply for himself. All these factors are important to you in choosing your words.

Clear Emphatic Words

Since—to continue Aristotle's convenient analysis— your *object* in using the spoken word is to explain, to describe, or to persuade, you should cultivate certain virtues, or qualities. The first and most important is *clarity*. You may have every other virtue as a speaker, but unless you are clear, the other virtues are useless. To alter the words of St. Paul when he defended the primacy of love to the Corinthians, without clarity you are sounding brass or a tinkling cymbal! Your first principle in choosing words, then, is that they be instantly, immediately clear to your hearers. The second virtue is *force* or *emphasis*. The force or emphasis should be inherent in the words or symbols you select; it should not depend merely upon the tone in which you utter the word. For instance, *battle* is a vigorous word. It is a more forceful symbol than *struggle, conflict,* or *engagement*. It even sounds stronger. A third virtue to cultivate in choosing words is *euphony*. The combinations of sound should be pleasant to the ear. The tongue twisters of your youth suggest that certain syllables are either harsh sounding or difficult to pronounce when they are combined. As an individual you may have difficulty with *f*'s, or *l*'s, or *r*'s, or *th*'s. If you have, you should avoid laying traps for yourself in your speech. Some words in combination produce expressions which are difficult to say and at the same time are unpleasant to the ear. It is fatally easy to fall into a succession of words with the same suffix: "This expression of opinion led to a proliferation of dissention." Shifts in vowel sounds can also lead to awkward or unpleasant combinations: Naval novel, bitter battle, wretched wrath are examples of this type of error. Alexander Pope provided both excellent advice and built-in examples concerning the sound of words. His reference was to writing, but it is applicable to speech as well.

True ease in writing comes from art, not chance,
As those move easiest who have learned to dance.
'Tis not enough no harshness gives offense,
The sound must seem an echo to the sense.
Soft is the strain when Zephyr gently blows,
And the smooth stream in smoother numbers flows;

But when loud surges lash the sounding shore,
The hoarse, rough verse should like the torrent roar;
When Ajax strives some rock's vast weight to throw,
The line too labors, and the words move slow.

A study of Pope's choice of words here is profitable. The sounds are directly related to the meaning, and they enhance it. You might note particularly the differing effects of monosyllabic and polysyllabic words when he wishes to produce force and vigor. The final virtue is the *grace* or *harmony* with which you combine words. It is quite possible to choose your individual words with care, yet to be awkward or incongruous in combining them. A jeweler may have fine stones to work with, but they will not show to advantage unless he designs a necklace in which the position of each gem enhances the brilliance of the others. So you must take pains that the words you choose as symbols combine harmoniously and gracefully to produce the larger idea you are attempting to shape.

Levels of Meaning

Your choice of words will be affected by two levels of meaning: the denotative and the connotative. The *denotation* of a word can be found in any good dictionary. But a word of caution is necessary here. When you check a doubtful word in your dictionary—and you should have one at your elbow when you prepare a speech—be sure you understand the system employed by that dictionary. Some provide definitions in historical order; others place the most common definition in the first position. Unless you remain aware of the system used by your dictionary, you may convey a meaning you do not really intend. Whereas the denotation of a word is the symbol limited by definition, the *connotation* consists of the accompanying symbols which time and custom and civilization have attached to the word. Some words are rich in connotation; some are poor. It is usually the common, simple words which are the richest in association. Two common examples are *home* and *father*. If the word *home* is contrasted with *domicile, residence, lodging*, and even *dwelling*, the difference is clear. *Home* at once suggests family, friends, cherished possessions, memories of people and events, a special street, or a remembered countryside. None of the other words bring those ideas with them. *Father* can be defined as *male parent, sire, progenitor*, even as the inflated *paternal ancestor*. But none of the synonyms have the profound suggestions which come from human relations, religion, and patriotism which live in the word *father*. Among the many echoes from that word are the Lord's Prayer; Washington, the Father of his Country; Fatherland; the reciprocal love of father and son; and a host of others. In choosing your words, then, you will be sensitive to the connotative effect which is so important in stirring a response from your audience. You will avoid the cold, inflated word in favor of the simple, direct word which has so many associations to enrich and to support it.

While a good abridged dictionary will suffice for definition, for connotation an unabridged dictionary is the reliable source. However, you will probably find that Roget's *Thesaurus* is more convenient for checking connotation and for providing a source for alternative wordings. As you employ the dictionary and the *Thesaurus*, you will find that to an increasing degree your skill in speaking will "come from art, not chance." You will be surer of the precise effect your words will have upon your audience. Another excellent guide to accurate, sensitive choice of words is Fowler's *Modern English Usage*. It is a witty, clear, and powerful antidote to shoddy and pretentious diction.

Abstract and Concrete Words

In addition to the denotative and connotative effects of your words, there are other factors which influence your choice. One of these is the distinction between abstract and concrete terms. While it is true that many of the great words in the language are abstract—*justice, honor, love, patriotism, faith, art, science*—they are comprehensive in their meanings. Yet, it is your prime duty to be clear, to control the imaginations of your hearers. If you are not careful to define the exact area involved in your use of an abstract word, you and your audience may part mental company. Therefore, when you employ an abstract term, you should illustrate it. If you speak of justice, do you refer to the law, to some form of social justice, to economic justice, to a correct opinion about a person's conduct? The context of your remarks alone may not establish the area with sufficient precision. One failure to establish a firm control over the range of your hearer's imaginations may not be serious. But this failure is such a common error that you should be sensitive to it.

General terms, as distinct from *abstract* words, offer many of the same hazards with much less excuse for them. If you wish to test the truth of this point, you might ask a group of friends to tell you the image that leaps to the mind of each one when you repeat a word. Then say *dog, house, automobile,* or *tree.* The breed and size of each dog; the size, color, and design of each house; the make and color of each car; and the size and species of each tree will differ with almost every individual. Had you said *Irish setter, white cottage, Cadillac,* or *maple,* the differences between the images produced in each mind would be insignificant. You should, then, employ symbols with as clear outlines as possible. Since people learn through their senses, words which convey definite sense impressions have a strong and immediate appeal. They also control the hearer's imagination without his being aware of that control. If you are discussing a tax structure which regards an automobile as a luxury, you can speak generally of the effect on patrons of the automotive industry. Or you can discuss the effect on buyers of Chevrolets, Midwestern Gasoline, and Tread-well Tires. The concrete words will keep the minds of your audience from wandering into irrelevant segments of the automotive industry and from viewing your point as theory only distantly related to actuality.

Words as Land-Marks

Furthermore, your audience will influence your choice of words as it influences your manner and your organization. For instance, with one audience you may use technical terms without hesitation. With a second, you may scatter technical words throughout your speech, but you must define those you use. In preparing for the third audience, you might well decide to avoid technical terms entirely. Your choice of terms will be guided by your knowledge that people have two vocabularies—active and latent. Their active vocabulary consists of words they use correctly and comfortably in speech and writing. Their latent vocabulary is made up of words which they recognize when they see or hear them, but which they are not likely to employ themselves. As a speaker you must recognize the latent vocabulary; otherwise you will talk down to your audience. On the other hand, the degree of recognition is important for your choice. Consider a miscellaneous set of terms: *vector, quantum theory, transcendentalism, balance of payments, laissez-faire, open-end fund.* To some people one or more of those words will summon a rich background of associations and information. They will understand the precise meaning of the term, and they will see the term in its expanded significance. For other people some of the words will convey a general idea. They will recognize the word as belonging to physics or literature or economics, but cannot define the concept except in very broad terms. For some people, finally, one or more of the terms will be without meaning at all. They cannot trust themselves to place these terms in even a broad category. In choosing your words, you must estimate the level of your audience if you are to communicate effectively.

There is no greater artistry than the ability to express complex ideas and abstruse technical concepts in language which is clear to the layman.

Suiting Your Words to the Audience

For some speeches you will prepare a written text so that you will have ample time to perfect your wording. On other occasions you may speak from notes. Your choice of words when you speak from notes is no less important than your choice when you write your speech. In some ways, it is more important. Your notes provide a topical guide. But as you rehearse your speech, you should establish a series of key words which develop each topic, which lead from one topic to the next, and which give emphasis, color, and point to your illustrations. Having established these words as landmarks, you can maintain the pace and order of your remarks. You will not be caught groping for a word at a critical point in your speech. A glance at the recorded speeches in the chapters on beginning a speech and on developing the thought will illustrate what happens when insufficient thought has been given to the wording. Repetition, inflated phrasing, unresolved generalities are all too common. The advantage of speaking from notes is that you are free and direct in confronting your audience. But that freedom and confidence can come only when you are assured that each important word will appear when you summon it. Words which are vital to the effect you wish to convey should perhaps be included in your notes.

Varying the Combinations

But it is not enough to choose individual words which are rich in connotation, which appeal to the senses, and which are strong and exact in meaning; you must also combine them effectively. Like the famous division of Gaul into three parts, sentences can be classified in three ways: the *loose*, the *periodic*, and the *balanced*. Each produces its peculiar effect. The *loose* sentence is the most common variety. Its essential meaning is completed before the sentence ends: "The President delivered a message to Congress, which had been summoned to hear it." Any sentence which has explanatory or qualifying material occurring after the main thought has been presented falls into this category. A loose sentence lacks special emphasis. On the other hand, not every sentence can be emphatic, nor should it be. An army cannot all be officers. In the *periodic* sentence the meaning is not complete until the end; hence there is a climax. You will note, of course, that the meaning of the sentence is not changed if the thought is expressed as: "When he considered the political climate favorable, the President summoned Congress." But the *effect* is quite different. You should seriously consider, then, putting your important ideas in periodic form. The audience will not be aware of your technique, but they will be influenced by it. Periodic sentences should be used consciously at the beginning and at the end of each segment of your speech. You will probably have fewer occasions to use the *balanced* sentence: "To devise such a system may take months; to develop it, years." This sentence poises or contrasts two ideas by using identical structure and word order on each side of the semicolon. The balanced sentence is rather formal for contemporary style, yet it is dramatic. You may find it useful when you are seeking an unusually emphatic beginning or ending for one of your topics.

The length of sentences as well as their form is important to you as a speaker. As a general rule, the sentences in a speech should be shorter than those in a piece of normal prose. This distinction is most important if you are speaking from a manuscript. Long, intricate sentences are difficult to read aloud. You may become lost in qualifying phrases and fail to give the central idea sufficient emphasis. You may simply run out of breath. Your sentences must be designed for ease in speaking and frequently for ease in reading as well. You should, then, vary the length of your sentences. Short sentences produce two effects: emphasis and speed. A short sentence is almost always emphatic when it occurs in contrast to longer sentences. A series of short sentences sacrifices some of the emphasis but produces speed. Caesar's famous "I came, I saw, I conquered" is a good example. Too many short sentences, however, produce the style of the primer and negate both emphasis and rapid movement. They represent the worst form of talking down to your audience. Longer sentences express more complex thoughts. Since much of what you say will be complex in its very nature, you will have to use some reasonably long sentences. It is not difficult, however, to keep them within reasonable bounds. The simplest way is to come to a full stop when you are tempted to use *and* or *but*. This one device should keep your sentences short enough to read without strain and without breathlessness. So if you regard your speaking as an art and if you are aware that you can become more proficient in that art, you will exercise a conscious control over the length and the variety of the sentences you use.

Jargon

By keeping your attention directed to clarity, emphasis, euphony, and grace, you will avoid jargon. This is the language of those who put words before thought, who wish to impress—not to make clear—who confuse obscurity with depth. It has been called "officialese," "gobbledygook," and other uncomplimentary names, yet it springs up everywhere. It arises in part from the mistaken notion that an invented vocabulary adds dignity or professionalism to some profession or business. It is, unfortunately, an attractive nuisance, because most people have a hankering to impress their fellows. The jargon expert goes about it the wrong way: He avoids the concrete word as he would the plague; he is more impressed by the length of a word than by its connotation; he has no sense of the rhythm and sound of a good sentence.

The English essayist and novelist George Orwell has written in jargon a well-known parody of a verse from Ecclesiastes.

I returned, and saw under the sun, that the race is not to the swift, nor the battle to the strong, neither yet bread to the wise, nor yet riches to men of understanding, nor yet favor to men of skill; but time and chance happeneth to them all.

Orwell's version is an accusatory finger pointed at far too many writers and speakers [1].

Objective consideration of contemporary phenomena compels the conclusion that success or failure in competitive activities exhibits no tendency to be commensurate with innate capacity, but that a considerable element of the unpredictable must be taken into account.

If you read both passages aloud, you will see at once that the passage from the Bible has a deep, natural rhythm so that both pauses and emphasis fall just where they should. The parody—words rather than meaning—is almost impossible to read aloud. The reader is lost in a cloud of inflated language which provides neither resting place nor guide to emphasis. You will at the same time observe that words such as *sun, race, battle, strong, bread, wise, riches, skill* are all short, concrete words. They are rich in connotations. *Objective consideration, contemporary phenomena, competitive activities* are abstract, cold, indecisive words. They do not control the imagination of the hearer. *Competitive activities* could be anything from the effort to secure a Ph.D. to a game of marbles. The writer of Ecclesiastes is expressing a very profound thought. Yet he does so largely through mono-

[1] From George Orwell, "Politics and the English language," in *Shooting an Elephant and Other Essays*, copyright 1945–1946–1949–1950 by Sonia Brownell Orwell, Harcourt, Brace & World, Inc., New York.

syllables. *Time* and *chance* are major concepts, and certainly they are abstract, but they are defined in homely and concrete terms: *race, battle, bread, riches.* This example of jargon, which is luminously clear beside some of the instructions to taxpayers prepared by the Internal Revenue Service, is language only distantly related to meaning. It is language characteristic of one who is thinking of himself—not his audience. He is preening himself on his knowledge of words and his ability to pronounce them correctly—not on the clear images he is producing in the minds of his hearers. *The Elements of Style,* by Strunk and White, is a brief but effective defense against jargon.

In choosing and in arranging your words, you should be moderate. Most words have come into the language because they serve a useful purpose. Therefore, they should be used when they are appropriate. You should neither make a point of using as many words of Anglo-Saxon derivation as possible nor become addicted to long words of Latin origin. A judicious mixture of the two is best—as Shakespeare proved. For the same reason you should take a middle ground both in the length and construction of your sentences. The point is that you should exercise a deliberate choice over your words and their arrangement. By refining your technique through the conscious discrimination between alternative wordings and alternative structures, you will exercise an increasingly sure control over your audience. You will be clear, emphatic, euphonious, and graceful.

A Summary

Finally a few very simple recommendations and warnings may alert you to common problems and dangers. You may feel sure that you are aware of them, but the best writers at times fall into the errors they represent. They may serve you as a convenient checklist.

Prefer the concrete to the general word. It establishes at once an identity of images in the hearer's and the speaker's minds. You can usually substitute *the New York Central* for *railroad* and by so doing provide associations in depth for your audience. Good writers and speakers use this technique constantly.

Use concrete illustrations or definitions with abstract words. When you speak of patriotism, do you refer to Lincoln's decision to put the cause of the Union above his chance for reelection, Nathan Hale's regret that he had but one life to give for his country, or the cynical definition that "patriotism is the last refuge of scoundrels"? The word itself might arouse any one of these suggestions in the minds of individual members of the audience.

Try to use strong verbs. A strong verb can carry in itself the force of a qualifying phrase. You may report that President Truman said something. But you may also say that he *retorted, declared, objected, insisted,* or *responded.* Each of these verbs indicates in some way the tone or the circumstances in which the words were uttered. In like manner you may say, "He did not like the policies established by his successor." Verbs which would indicate either his state of mind or the degree of his disfavor might be *loathed, detested, despised, ab- horred, scorned, deplored,* or *denigrated.*

Acronyms and abbreviations should be explained at least once. You cannot be sure that everyone in the audience knows at once what NASA, SEC, AMA, or ICC means. If you give the full name once, you may then safely refer to the initials subsequently. As acro- nyms become more and more popular, there is an in- creasing need to identify them.

Except in static description, prefer the active to the passive voice. The passive voice does not lend itself to emphasis: "It was seen by General Cannon that the situ- ation was critical, and so he acted upon it." A much stronger version would be to say: "General Cannon saw the critical situation and acted." The passive voice en- courages wordiness, and it leads to illogical and ridiculous statements such as: "Crossing the street, her purse was dropped." Her purse was not crossing the street under its own power.

Avoid trite and hackneyed expressions. A cliché is simply an expression which was so memorable that it lost its effectiveness through overuse. You should be sus- picious of using phrases which have a familiar ring. It is fatally easy to stitch together a fabric of tired phrases as you prepare your remarks. The phrases become almost automatic—add insult to injury, bolt out of the blue, red as a rose, each and every, at sixes and sevens, needs no introduction, gild the lily—the list could go on indefi- nitely. Train your ear to recognize them and avoid them.

Avoid stringing phrases together until meaning and

emphasis are lost. Qualifiers of your principal thought may, like the Arab's camel in the fable, oust that thought from the sentence: "Visible was the roof of a house on top of a hill which lay at a distance to his left." The sprawl of that sentence can be corrected simply: "In the distance he saw the roof of a house perched on a hilltop." Larger units of thought can fall into the same vagueness: "The president of the corporation was a man who could reach a quick decision on any question which arose as a result of changing methods which involved a change in the approach which salesmen use with their customers." This sentence is far worse than any you would compose, but it illustrates the fatal habit of tacking ideas on the sentence long after it has lost momentum. A simpler version does not omit many ideas: "The president of the corporation quickly decided questions —the result of changing methods—involving the approach of salesmen to their customers." A good rule of thumb is to make every word you use justify its presence in your speech or observations. In particular avoid wordy expressions such as "throughout the whole world." The idea gains nothing from being expressed twice.

Chapter 11
MECHANICS OF DELIVERY

> O wad some Power the giftie gie us
> To see oursels as ithers see us!

Robert Burns might well be speaking to every man who has had occasion to address his fellows. It is true that your audience, large or small, is chiefly concerned with *what* you have to say. At the same time, if their minds are open and receptive, so are their eyes. As you are speaking, those eyes are estimating you as a person. In the minds of that audience the evidence supplied by the eyes influences the evidence supplied by the ears. They judge you by how you appear as well as by what you are saying.

How do you appear to an audience? You should, of course, be your normal, warm, genial, interested self. But does an unconscious, intent frown as you concentrate on your words suggest to them that you are basically a rather grim fellow? Do you assume a rigidly severe expression in the hope that you will appear calm and self-contained, while the audience is regarding you as a wooden image, a stick? Do you speak at the audience rather than with them? All these unfortunate, and actually false, attitudes may be conveyed quite unconsciously. After all, you know that you are an easy, friendly, congenial person; but it is important that the audience know it also. If you do much speaking, it would be wise to have a friend take movies as you speak or as you rehearse. Everyone knows how strange one's recorded voice sounds when one hears it for the first time. You may experience the same sense of shock when you see on a screen how you appear to others. A mirror does not convey the same effect at all, because if you rehearse before a mirror you can only half concentrate on what you are saying; so you may not observe the effect you produce when you are actually concentrating on your speech.

Your object, then, is to be relaxed and conversational as you speak. That attitude will allow you to bring the full weight of your personality, your conviction, your animation, and your humor to the support of your topic. There are certain techniques which will help you to achieve these effects, and there are a number of mannerisms you should avoid.

Eye Contact

My Bishop's eyes I've never seen,
Though the light in them may shine.
For when he prays, he closes his,
And when he preaches, mine!
(Anonymous)

This verse records a common result of lack of eye contact. For eye contact is the most significant element in the delivery of a speech. Whether you are talking to an individual during an interview, to 10 men at a conference table, or to 500 people in an auditorium, you should direct your remarks to the person or persons whom you are addressing. Each listener should have the impression that you are speaking directly to him. Looking at the members of an audience, whether they are a large group or a small gathering at a conference table, appears to be a simple matter. Yet many experienced speakers neglect this fundamental technique. They look at the floor, at the ceiling, at the sides of the room, over the heads of the audience, or out a window. Even when the speaker's eyes are directed toward his listeners, he may have a fixed stare which looks through, rather than directly at, them.

A speaker may often begin by employing good eye contact, but if he hesitates momentarily, searching for a word or phrase he is not certain of, he gives himself away by turning his eyes from the audience. They at once sense his uncertainty. But if he keeps good eye contact—even though he may pause for some time—they will credit him with thinking on his feet. He, in turn, will find that the word or phrase he needs is more likely to come to his mind—for his control of the audience has not been lost. At the same time, he should not appear to be a spectator at a tennis match, his eyes turning from right to left in a regular rhythm. Rather his eyes should move easily and naturally from one segment of the audience to another.

You must, however, beware of that member of an audience who shows his approval of what you are saying by a pleased smile or a nod of his head. You may be so gratified by the response of this admirably perceptive person that you direct your eyes to him for the rest of your speech. It is important not to favor even one segment of your audience, much less an individual! You owe as much attention to those sitting at the sides of the room as to those in the middle. Your thoughtfulness in sharing your interest with each section of the audience will be rewarded as they, in turn, give you their undivided attention. Oral communication with a live audience is the one occasion when the exchange is truly reciprocal. The facial expressions, the nods, even an intent hush bring an immediate and gratifying reward to the speaker. This, in turn, further warms and animates him so that he speaks with deeper conviction and greater relaxation. The stimulus to his confidence releases any tensions he may have felt originally.

Eye contact, then, is a major technique in establishing a close mutual exchange between speaker and audience. One other should be mentioned briefly. You cannot communicate unless you can be heard, and you cannot speak conversationally if your voice beats at the ears of your audience. Whether you use a microphone or not, you should be sure that your voice is so pitched that it will be audible to those in the back rows without seeming strident to those in front. If you do use a microphone, you must be careful that in maintaining eye contact with various parts of your audience, you do not move too far from the microphone itself. Nothing makes an audience more restless than not hearing what the speaker is saying.

Nervous Mannerisms

Even the most experienced speakers are tense before they deliver an address; professional athletes, actors, and actresses are subject to the same nervous strain. But the difference between the experienced and the inexperienced speaker, between the professional and the amateur, is that the experienced person has learned to conceal and control his tension. His air of calm confidence, of ease, assures the audience that he is in control of the situation and of his subject.

There are three ways in which you can build an inner confidence and at the same time present a poised, relaxed appearance to an audience: first, by having a genuine enthusiasm for your subject matter; second, by having your thoughts thoroughly organized; and third, by avoiding mannerisms which reveal inner tenseness and insecurity! As the American psychologist William James pointed out, action begets and increases emotion. A man may run because he is afraid, but the act of running increases his fear. Thousands of people who have attended classes in speaking will remember vividly how their initial nervousness was increased as their state of mind became manifest to their audience.

More than any other part of your body, your hands may reveal your inner tensions. If you keep them relaxed and under control, you have gone a long way toward presenting a calm, assured appearance to your audience.

*Playing with Sugar Bowl. A speaker should refrain
from manipulating objects on the table. He may look
at the object he is handling and lose eye contact with
his audience. The audience is likely to watch him
rather than to listen to him. The speaker's insecurity,
which is manifested by his fiddling with the sugar
bowl, is not concealed by his too negligent posture
and by the distracting display of shirt front.*

Therefore, avoid (1) holding them behind your back,
(2) putting them in your pockets, (3) clasping and
wringing them, (4) clenching your fists, (5) scratching
your head or touching your face, (6) twisting a coat
button, (7) adjusting your necktie, and (8) constantly
removing your spectacles. Any of these actions—of
which you may be quite unconscious—distracts your
audience. And by revealing your inner uncertainty, they
diminish the vigor and conviction of the material in your
speech. Equally important is the fact that these same
distractions subconsciously make the speaker himself
nervous.

There are other mannerisms which have the same effect. Falling into awkward postures and restless shifting of the feet are two of them. Others have to do with the voice. Filling pauses with *er*'s and *ah*'s or indulging in nervous coughs are evidences of tension and disturb your audience. Winston Churchill showed both by precept and by example how effective a pause can be. Your audience has no means of knowing that a pause was not intended to produce an effect. But the inexperienced speaker is so terrified by a pause that he attempts to fill it either with sound or with physical action.

By controlling the mannerisms which reveal an inner uncertainty and tension, you fortify what confidence you have, and at the same time you impress your audience. You should be comforted by the knowledge that the most experienced public performers share your initial apprehension, though they do not reveal it to their audiences. After fourteen years with the Cleveland Browns,

Scratching Head and Pulling Ear. During a pause in a speech or when he is reaching for a word, a speaker may scratch his head or tug at his ear. Such movements reveal his lack of confidence and self-possession.

Hands Clasped in Front. Clasping the hands in front of him, the speaker assumes a hunched posture. The tenseness in his hands is communicated to his speech and is obvious to his audience. He should let his hands hang loosely at his sides or rest lightly on the table, if it is high enough.

Lou Groza was asked if he was still nervous when he ran on the field. He replied that his stomach was tied in knots whenever he went into a game and that when this condition was no longer true he would give up football. In *The Ape in Me*, Cornelia Otis Skinner reports that the greatest actresses and actors have suffered abject stage fright before their first entrance. She mentions a famous French comedienne who had to be thrust on the stage physically, but who invariably gave a superb performance.

When you learn to control the mannerisms which can

betray your inner state of mind to your audience, you will gain both satisfaction and confidence: satisfaction because mastering one's emotions is always gratifying, and confidence because the response of the audience will be so rewarding.

To gain this control two things are necessary: first, a self-analysis to reveal the particular mannerisms into which you fall during moments of stress, and second, practice under the eye of your wife, or some equally critical friend, until avoiding the mannerisms is natural for you. However, since a direct, easy delivery is your goal, you should take care that in avoiding the dangers of nervous mannerisms, you do not fall into the equal danger of self-consciousness.

Folded Arms. Folding the arms indicates tension and prevents natural gestures. Here the speaker is unable to complete the gesture which the left hand seeks to initiate.

Chapter 12

SUITING THE ACTION TO THE WORD

Taken in small doses, Hamlet's advice to the players about suiting the word to the action and the action to the word is excellent advice. Like an actor, a speaker has the attention of an audience focused upon him. He must project both his voice and his character, and he must evoke a response in the audience. For these reasons you, as a speaker, must be conscious of your movements and gestures. For if you are *not* conscious of them, instinctive, but awkward or poorly timed, gestures may have an unfortunate effect upon your speech.

The Function of Gesture

A gesture may be defined as a motion of any part of the body intended to lend emphasis or color to the words being spoken. Gesture may be extremely expressive. Certain art forms, notably ballet and the mime, depend entirely upon bodily movement to convey meaning. For the speaker, however, movement and gesture should be occasional adjuncts to an art which depends almost entirely on words. Gesture has been made suspect largely through the mistaken efforts of the old-time elocution teachers, whose exaggerated and hackneyed gestures are quite rightly subject to ridicule. However, in escaping the dangers of trite and excessive gesture, you may be tempted to run to the other extreme. Complete absence of gesture reduces you to a robot, a talking machine. In the eyes of the audience, you lose your humanity, your force of character and personality. You appear either perfunctory or frightened into rigidity. Therefore, when you speak, you must be aware both of the gestures you intend to use and of the gestures you may use unconsciously. The instinctive gesture may well be the best one and most appropriate for your purpose; on the other hand, it may be one which detracts from your effect rather than enhances it. The point is that you must be alert to what you are doing as well as to what you are saying.

Gestures may serve as effective visual aids in the descriptive phases of your talk. Airplane pilots are prone to use their hands graphically to describe two planes maneuvering or to show the angle of bank or glide. An engineer may use his hands or arms to translate the inches or centimeters of a piece of apparatus into dimensions which the audience grasps at once. For many people besides fishermen, the concept of 14 inches can be an elastic one. The gesture provides an image of an actual space. A lawyer appealing to a jury may use similar gestures to remind them of the precise circumstances of an automobile accident. These physical movements catch the imagination of the audience and give them the momentary illusion that they are actually viewing what the speaker is describing.

But the gestures also have an important secondary effect on you as a speaker. They tend to relax whatever nervous tension you may have. Anyone who has had athletic experience knows that physical movement dissipates tension. Batters waiting for a pitch move the bat until the last possible moment in order to remain completely relaxed and loose. Even slight physical movement as you speak will produce a similar result. Tension in one part of the body produces tension all over; so relaxation of one part tends to relax the whole. A few simple gestures will provide enough movement to bring about ease of posture and a confident appearance. But it follows logically that gestures must be natural and apparently spontaneous if they are to convey a relaxed attitude and yet give color and emphasis to your words. The term *apparently spontaneous* may seem to be contradictory, yet most arts—painting, sculpture, poetry—strive to achieve outward spontaneity while maintaining a strict inner control—and speaking is an art. Practical suggestions in the use of gesture, therefore, fall into the general area of control.

Using and Misusing Your Hands

The first suggestion is that you be no more repetitious in your gestures than in your words. Although the range of gesture is far smaller than the range of words, you need not repeat the *same* gesture in close succession. Even skillful speakers fall victim to this error. The late President Kennedy used a jabbing motion with his right hand to the extent that the gesture sometimes obtruded on what he was saying and proved a distraction rather than an emphasis. Overuse of a prodding or pointing motion of the hand also jeopardizes eye contact with the audience, for the speaker's eye tends to follow the direction of his hand. The second point is to avoid abrupt or jerky gestures. When you use your hands, let the whole arm come up gracefully. Then as the hand movement is completed, your arms drop slowly to your side or to the lectern. Control of this simple action seems to give speakers a degree of confidence which is surprising in view of the simplicity of the motion. Whenever you do bring your hands into play, be very sure that they are raised high enough to be visible to the audience. Otherwise the audience becomes conscious only of vague, unrelated movements on your part. Abortive gestures are worse than no gestures at all. Speakers are often impelled to use a natural and effective motion of the hands, but they check the impulse with a nervous flick of the wrist or an opening and closing of the fingers—the common "milking gesture"—neither of which motions has any significance to the audience.

There are a few additional suggestions for the effective use of your hands. The first of these is that you gain variety by sometimes using one hand and sometimes using two. Certain gestures with the hands may be instinctive with you. Because they are instinctive, they are probably right and natural, but because you should also control your gestures, you must seek variety. Without establishing a fixed pattern, you should make use of your left hand as well as your right, both hands as well as one. But however desirable and effective gestures with both hands may be, there is one which may lead you into difficulty if you misuse it. In enumerating points or examples, a speaker may hold up the appropriate number of fingers. At point one he grasps one finger—then forgets to let go. As a result he immobilizes his hands so that point two cannot be emphasized, nor can any intervening gestures be made no matter how appropriate they might be. A gesture becomes awkward when it is either sustained too long or repeated too often. Furthermore, gestures should develop naturally in your speech. Give your audience a little time to accept your unadorned personality before you begin to accent it with gesture. As they warm to you, your gestures will seem a natural expression of your true self. Introduced too early in your speech, they may seem theatrical and so detract from the air of conviction you wish to establish.

When you are not using your hands, they should hang loosely at your side, or rest lightly on the lectern. From either of these positions they can move easily and naturally into the audience's view. With the hands in these positions you will be inclined to use them more frequently and more appropriately. When your hands are locked behind your back or buried in your pockets, it requires too much effort to extricate them; so gesture is inhibited. The same situation holds when you fold your arms.

The fact that gesture can seem spontaneous and moving and at the same time be conscious and controlled is illustrated by the late distinguished actor George Arliss. When he left the stage for the last time (in the role of Shylock), he trailed a hand behind him in a gesture that moved the audience deeply. What the audience could not see was that his other hand was reaching for the cards in his interrupted bridge game. It is only sound technique which can produce the confidence and control of a George Arliss.

Facial Expression

However, his hands are not the only physical means by which a speaker affects an audience. The expression on his face is a screen on which the audience will read, or appear to read, a reflection of the inner man. Whether they read your real character accurately depends upon whether your expression is a reflection of your sincerity, warmth, and conviction, or whether it is a reflection of the strain and tension imposed by the circumstances. In any event the audience will begin to read your expression from the moment that you approach the rostrum. You should, then, compose yourself so that from the first moment you appear, you are your best and most natural self. You should not handicap yourself by having to break down an original impression of insecurity or coldness or superficiality. But in conveying a warm and vibrant personality, you must not fall into an image of genial warmth which you maintain at all costs. There are times when you must be forceful. Your facial expression must, in some degree, echo the tone and implications of your words.

The symphony conductor uses his hands or baton to control the rhythm of his orchestra and to bring in the different instruments at their appointed times. The speaker uses his hands to provide emphasis and visual imagery for his words. But anyone who has watched a symphony on television has been struck by the control exercised by the conductor's facial expressions. These evoke a response from the musicians which lifts what could be a routine performance to a moving, emotional experience. In like manner, the overtones, the nuances of a speech, are often controlled or enhanced by a speaker's change of expression. The speaker's expression must change to fit the import of his words. If the skillful choice of words and a beautiful speaking voice were enough, then the genius of a great writer; the moving, resonant voice of a distinguished actor; and the range and depth of a stereophonic instrument could be combined to produce an ideal speech. Experience shows that this synthesis does not work in practice. Beautiful sounds conveying splendid ideas are still coming from a machine. One live, vibrant, unique human being is not setting up an interaction with a group of his fellows.

Inexperienced speakers tend to overlook this aspect of a speech. They are so intent upon what they have to say that they take little heed of the impression they are making on their audience. While it is fatal to become self-conscious, you should give thought to your facial expression. It should always be relaxed and friendly, because by being relaxed, it will be sufficiently mobile to conform to the sense of what you are saying. It should be friendly because what you project is likely to be returned to you. It is neither necessary nor appropriate to arrange your features in a fixed and affable smile; your eyes can do more than anything else to convey your warm, lively interest in your audience.

In the course of a number of speech classes, an interesting experiment was repeated. One of the class sessions was regularly devoted to recording on sound film a speech by every member of the class. As each speaker appeared before the microphone and camera, he was asked to say a few words as a test of his voice. The results were usually light attempts at humor: "It couldn't happen to a better guy!" "This is my greatest moment." "Wait until my wife sees this."

During these remarks, the speakers were completely relaxed and natural. They were warm and friendly. However, as soon as the cameraman said, "We are now ready for the speech," the casual, friendly look changed to one of apprehension at best, and sheer terror at worst. What the speaker did not know was that his preliminary remarks as well as his speech were being recorded. When these men saw the films projected, they were shocked by the abrupt change of personality which appeared on the screen. Their Jekyll-and-Hyde performance offered them dramatic proof that their image of themselves and their image as it appeared to the audience were in sharp contrast. So every speaker *must* give serious thought to the impression he is making on an audience.

Finally, your facial expression must convey the impression that speaking to the specific audience before you gives you real pleasure. If your expression and attitude do not indicate that you are enjoying yourself, how can the audience be expected to find pleasure in what you have to say? Even a speech which is purely informative can give pleasure, because most people like to pass from ignorance to knowledge. But you, as a speaker, must show by your very appearance that you enjoy sharing that knowledge. Only by paying attention to how you appear to the audience can you gain the great satisfaction that comes from the reciprocal human exchange that occurs between a good speaker and good audience.

Chapter 13

DON'T SPEAK TO ME IN THAT TONE OF VOICE

During the long ages which preceded the invention of the public-address system, radio, and television, the demands on a speaker's voice were such that he required almost the same training as a professional singer. The traveling evangelist, the public lecturer, the political candidate, to name but a few, regularly spoke to large crowds and often spoke out of doors. Typically the people came to the speaker. He never came to their homes by means of radio or television. As a result, he had to learn to project his voice so that it could be heard— and heard distinctly—in the far reaches of an auditorium or at the outer fringes of a large crowd in the out-of-doors. He needed advanced technical training in voice production, articulation, projection, resonance, and breath control. A speech of any length was a severe test of physical endurance. Edward Everett's two-hour speech delivered at Gettysburg was an amazing exhibition of stamina for speaker and audience alike.

Fortunately for today's speaker, he can talk to several hundred people in a high school auditorium or to several thousand people in a municipal stadium using little physical effort. Thanks to the microphone and the amplifier, he can speak in a natural, conversational tone and still be heard distinctly by every section of his audience. Neither his voice nor his lungs are under any strain. Oratory—in its accepted sense—went out when amplification came in.

At the same time, the advent of the microphone does not mean that clear, distinct articulation and effective tone control can be neglected. Although the overly dramatic enunciation and exaggerated variation of tone which characterized the professional orator have become the subject of humor—and properly so—the precision of diction and the flexibility of tone represented by the tradition are still valid aims for a speaker. It is simply that mechanical has replaced physical amplification of voice so that professional techniques and practices of control are no longer necessary. On the other hand, mechanical amplification makes slurred or garbled words and uncertain or inappropriate tone painfully apparent. With complete impartiality, an electronic system magnifies the good and bad qualities of the human voice. It is still necessary to learn and to practice good techniques, but these are neither so elaborate nor so demanding as they were in former times.

The speaker trained under the rigid formulas of the professional elocutionist tended to become a stereotype—to lose the accent and the turns of phrase which proclaimed him an individual. The late President Kennedy made no attempt to reduce his distinctive New England accent to the flat norm of an announcer on television. He was an effective speaker because he dared to be himself. Senator Dirksen's rolling periods are often parodied, but he never lacks an audience because his tone and delivery are perfectly natural for him. He has a style which is at once distinctive and appropriate. Since oral communication is always a person-to-person relationship, techniques to improve the speaker's voice production should never interfere with the qualities which establish him as an individual.

The Essential Qualities of the Voice

But the voice is a musical instrument as well as a mode of communicating thought. It can be pleasing or harsh, animated or dull. Four qualities determine its effect on an audience: pitch, volume, rhythm, and articulation. Neglecting any one of these fundamentals detracts from the impression the speaker wishes to make, for he appeals to the minds of his audience through their ears. If their ears are offended by harshness or stridency of pitch and volume, dulled by monotony of rhythm, or strained by poor articulation, he creates a poor channel for the flow of thought. Attention to these four qualities does open wide the stream of communication and establishes the speaker as an animated, convincing, warm, and modest person.

If you regard your voice as a musical instrument, you

should become familiar with its range and flexibility. You should know in what register it produces its most pleasing effect and how far above or below that register it can go without strain or harshness. Much has been written about tone production, but most of the material applies to a singer rather than to a speaker. Yet the demands of each are similar rather than identical. A singer, for instance, must sustain a tone for a number of seconds; the speaker must produce the tone but does not have to sustain it. Hence the singer must devote study and practice to resonance and breath control which as a speaker you may safely neglect.

For example, the familiar *Lord's Prayer* by Malotte requires a singer to produce and sustain pure tones for a considerable length of time in the opening phrases. The speaker utters the same phrases in two or three seconds. Again in the Bach-Gounod arrangement of *Ave Maria*, a phrase which can be read in eight seconds takes fifteen to sing. For most speakers, then, a few suggestions and some time spent in practice with a tape recorder will suffice to establish the range and quality of their voices. If you find difficulties, however, which moderate practice does not overcome, you should then consult a speech specialist. Some problems of tone or articulation may be beyond your own analysis and treatment. Otherwise, critical attention to the sound of your own voice on tape and an understanding of the common difficulties which beset the voices of speakers should enable you to master control of your voice as an instrument.

Having used a tape recorder to find the register to which your voice is best suited and the range through which it can easily move, you should then check your voice for the weaknesses or errors to which most speakers are prone. The following suggestions will indicate possible trouble spots in each of the four aspects of good voice production. As you learn to control your voice, you will employ calculated rather than random sound to make your speaking more effective.

Pitch

It is a common experience that nervousness and tension elevate the pitch of your voice. During very exciting moments, announcers at athletic events too often raise their pitch until they become unintelligible. If, then, you tend to be nervous at the beginning of a speech, you are likely to pitch your voice too high. The remedy lies in recognizing the possibility and in consciously lowering pitch to give you subsequent flexibility. High pitch works both ways. It reveals your tenseness and excitement, but it also rouses the same emotions in your audience. A moderate lifting of your pitch at appropriate times will stir and excite them. But at no time should you become strident in trying to be stimulating.

An excessively low pitch at the beginning often betrays overconfidence, and it has just as limiting an effect as its opposite. Continued too long, a low pitch sounds dull. On the other hand, it does suggest weight and importance. Dropping the pitch is as effective a way to produce emphasis as raising it. These factors suggest that your pitch at the beginning should be your most natural one, so that you can raise or lower it at will within the normal range of your voice.

Volume

Pitch and volume are related but not identical. Speaking more loudly than usual normally raises the pitch; so in increasing volume you must exercise care that you do not raise pitch at a time when you do not intend to do so. But your major problem with volume will probably come at the end of long phrases or sentences. A gradually diminishing volume produces a diminishing emphasis. Yet the important part of a sentence often comes at the end. You have already been reminded that a speech should be composed with natural breaks, so that you can sustain a consistent strength of voice to the very end of each thought. A sudden lowering of your voice is a fine way to obtain emphasis, but the whole idea should be spoken in lower tones, not just the last few words of a phrase.

Nervousness often produces a loud, forced tone which is unnatural for the speaker and unpleasant for the audience. The hammering of a stressed, resonant voice eventually affronts the ears of listeners, just as consistently low, mellow tones becoming deadening. You should, then, experiment with volume on the tape recorder. Observe what change in volume does to your voice, what upper and lower limits are likely to be unpleasant or indistinct. By a process of trial and error, you will find the range of volume which your voice can handle without strain or distortion. You should also make sure that you can change volume without losing the quality of your tone.

Rhythm

The importance of rhythm in speech may be illustrated by the fact that each language has its peculiar and characteristic stress and tempo. French differs from German in this respect—Italian from Swedish. People are apt to think that rhythm distinguishes poetry from prose, but the contrast is actually between a regular and an irregular stress. Poetry has a regular, measurable pattern of stress; prose also has patterns, but they are irregular.

However, when they are under emotional pressure, people tend to speak with an increasingly regular beat even in prose. English is capable of a great variety of rhythms; so you should take advantage of that potential as you speak.

Normally you will vary your tempo to suit the mood and importance of your thought. As in the other qualities involved in voice production, a middle ground will enable you to achieve variety in both directions. A nervous speaker tends to speak much too rapidly; an overcautious speaker moves at a pedestrian crawl. Both types are horrified when a pause occurs in their words and hasten to fill the silence with er's, ah's, coughs, or other nervous mannerisms. But occasional brief pauses are actually adjuncts to a speech especially when they herald a planned change in tempo.

Here again experiment with a tape recorder will indicate those parts of your speech which should move briskly and those in which a slower pace will provide weight and emphasis. You should bear in mind that your audience is not familiar with your thought. If you exceed 125 words a minute, your audience may find it difficult to translate your words into concepts. You may, therefore, find it advisable to use the tape recorder to check the number of words you are trying to crowd into a minute. You might also note whether your important, concluding ideas are spoken at a slower rate than merely illustrative material. The converse is equally important. Do you speak like a metronome? Do you give all your material the same rhythmic stress?

Like pitch and volume, rhythm adds color, variety, and emphasis to the speaking voice. You should use it consciously to enhance those parts of your speech where contrived pauses, regular stress, acceleration, or retardation will illuminate your meaning.

Articulation

The three previous elements of a good speaking voice concern words in groups and words in their context. Articulation deals with the individual word. It stresses the clear enunciation of the successive sounds which form a word and the correct placing of accent. Since a whole is no better than the parts that make it up, good articulation serves to improve pitch, volume, and rhythm.

Vowel sounds. The basic musical quality of English words lies in the five vowel sounds. When vowels are cut short or elided, even a carefully chosen word loses its color. Few people find difficulty in uttering the vowel sounds themselves; those that do so almost invariably fail to open their mouths wide enough to project clear sounds. If your voice on tape indicates muddy or blurred vowels, try speaking before a mirror. A rigid lower jaw which holds your teeth together tends to force the tone through your nose, thereby producing an objectionable and all too common nasal quality. A session before the mirror may lead you to relax your jaw, open your mouth, and produce a full, round tone.

You can eliminate most problems with vowel sounds if you will take time to give each one its full value. Haste, with resulting elision, is a common fault; for example:

po tent	po tnt
gov ern ment	gov mnt
sov er eign	sov rin
com pa ny	comp ny
lit er a ture	litra ture
im por tant	im por tnt
te di ous	te jus
in vi si ble	in vis ble
char ac ter is tic	char ac tris tic
con sid er able	con sid rable
per son nel	pers nel
tem per a ture	tem pra ture
con fer ence	con frence
sep a rate	se prate
soph o more	soph more
con tra dic tory	con tra dic try
con tem po ra ry	con temp a ry
mem o ry	mem ry
pow er ful	pow er fl

Reviewing and practicing the above words may remind you of how easy it is to neglect vowel sounds in polysyllabic words. However, your attention to the full and accurate sounding of vowels should not be exaggerated to the point of being stilted and pedantic.

Consonant sounds. Although clear vowel sounds are essential to good articulation, you must also sound your consonants distinctly. Failure to do so makes you rush your syllables and produces a slurred or garbled word. If you examine consonant sounds and their production, you will grasp their significance. For example, *p, d, g, t, b,* and *k* are strong consonants which give force to words. In each case a column of air is shut off as the consonant is formed and then the air is released suddenly. If the lips are not closed tightly, the firm *p* is lost. It should be sounded as in *puff*, so that if a lighted candle were placed in front of the mouth, the flame would flicker as you said the word. The word *power* when started with a good consonant sound is forceful, and the following vowel is accentuated. Here is a list of words to practice: The *p* sound: powerful, potent, parley, pillow, pungent, poor, pale, pile, peel, pole, pool. The *t* sound: tale, team, time, tall, tool. The *k* or hard *c* sound: case, keen, kind, cold, cool, quell, quick, question. The *d* sound: day, deal, die, dope, dupe. The *b* sound: base, beef, bite, bowl, boost. The *g* sound: gale, geese, guide, goal, good.

Both *m* and *n* are musical consonants and represent the humming quality of your voice. Yet this melodic potential is often neglected so that a dull, flat word results. The *m* sound: make, meek, mind, mold, music, mother, merry. The *n* sound: nail, need, nice, no, nude, never.

The consonant *h* is an aspirate and is accentuated in

laughter: ho, ho, ho or ha, ha, ha. Properly used the *h* sound opens your throat and mouth and allows the tone to originate from your diaphragm. It is one of the most neglected consonant sounds. When it is combined with *w*, it is frequently omitted. The *h* sound: hail, heel, high, home, hoop, hell, hull. The omitted *h*: wen instead of when, wether instead of whether, wat instead of what, and wistle instead of whistle.

The *v* sound is formed when the teeth and upper jaw come in contact with the lower lip. When this formation is hurried, the word becomes indistinct. The *v* sound: vain, veto, vibrant, vocal, vicious, victory, vigorous.

The sound of *f* is formed like that of *v*, except that the *f* sound begins with a stronger rush of air. The *f* sound: fade, feed, file, foam, food.

The *s* sound is sibilant and should not be overused, or it will produce an unpleasant whistling effect, especially through a public-address system. You must sound the *s*, but not sustain it. The *s* sound: sane, seen, size, sole, soon, sing.

One of the peculiarities of the English language is that most words end in consonants. Consonants used at the beginning of a word are followed by vowels which release whatever combinations of lip and tongue were needed for their formation. However, at the end of most words, there is a tendency not to release the consonant sound: for example, tight, gripe, rope, with, sloop, home, drive, cake, drift, drab, food, big, speak.

If the release of these consonants is exaggerated, the effect is theatrical. However, failure to release them results in a flat, indecisive tone. You must practice such words until you find a comfortable and attractive mean between the two extremes.

These suggestions and exercises are designed for those who recognize that improved articulation will increase the grace and power of their voices. A little practice with a tape recorder will often produce astonishing results. Most errors in pitch, volume, rhythm, and articulation are unconscious ones. If you note the errors which are commonly made and check your own performance with a critical ear, you may find that you have inadvertently fallen into one or two bad habits. A little corrective practice may produce a startling improvement in your speaking voice.

Chapter 14
HUMOR

Joking and humor are pleasant, and
often of extreme utility.
CICERO-*De Oratore*

For a man learns more quickly and
remembers more easily that which he
laughs at, than that which he approves
and reveres.
HORACE

Humor has a universal appeal. Like salt it heightens
flavor and makes what is digested by the mind more
palatable. But like salt, it should be used moderately and
appropriately. Unless the purpose of your speech is
simply to entertain, your humor should season only
those parts of your speech where it will enhance the total
effect. Too often speakers pay tribute to humor by beginning their speech with a contrived and often familiar
funny story, then resort to unrelieved seriousness for the
rest of the speech. You will be better advised to consider
some form of humor as an integral part of your talk.

There is always a danger that you may appear too serious to your audience. The deeper your conviction, the
more earnest your manner, the more this danger looms.
But touches of humor tell the audience that you do not

take yourself as seriously as you do your subject matter. A serious topic may make anyone seem pompous and didactic, an impression which a sense of humor cancels at once. These touches will form a bond between you and the audience—everyone prides himself on a sense of humor—so that you both share more completely in the substance of the speech because the approach to it is lightened.

Your humor should be as individual as you can make it. If it is to establish a bond with your audience, it should be characteristic of you as a person. So you should hesitate to borrow a funny story, even one which someone else has told with great success. The story may not fit you—and too many people may have heard it before. When the inappropriate story comes at the very beginning of the speech—"My being here this evening reminds me of a story. . . ."—a speaker may confuse his image just when he wants to impress it most firmly on the audience. On the other hand, you may be a person who tells stories very well. In which case the technique would work well for you. The point is that you should do only what you are sure you can do well.

One of the major functions of humor is to provide relief from emotional or intellectual tension. A little relaxation lets the mind come back to a problem with fresh concentration. No one understood audiences better than Shakespeare. Even in his most somber tragedies, he interjected humorous scenes, both to relieve the present tension and to make a great subsequent tension possible. Indeed one of these light scenes usually occurred just before the final calamity. Shakespeare released the mounting tension slightly, then developed it to the climax with fresh speed. Music, too, recognizes the same need. The scherzo was added to the original three movements of a symphony so that the seriousness of the work as a whole would be intensified by the lighter movement. Thus in developing your speech, you should consider at what points humor will provide the change of pace that will relax your audience and prepare them for the next major point.

It is easy to say that humor will improve your speech, but what form of humor? To answer that question you must take a realistic look at yourself. If your humor is to be successful it must be genuine, not forced. It must be appropriate both to the sort of person you are and to your topic as well. It must not offend the sensibilities of any member of your audience. The humor of the effervescent extrovert is not for the quiet, scholarly type. The converse is equally true, for attempts at humor rarely fall into a middle ground; either they succeed or they fall flat. One way to ensure failure is to misjudge the way you impress other people. One hazard lies in the fact that everyone is prone to admire the qualities of his opposite in temperament. Yet the exuberant personality who attempts the wry, understated wit of his introverted friend will fail in his effect because that type of humor does not conform to his nature. On the other hand, humor takes so many forms that everyone can find one which exactly suits his image. Even professional humorists usually cast themselves in a single role. You must simply make sure that the role you choose is one you can play naturally.

The Speaker as Victim

A role which will fit almost any personality is that of the *victim*. It arouses the sympathy of the audience and also lets each member of it feel slightly superior because he is sure he would never find himself in such an embarrassing situation. This type of humor may be represented by the plight of the dean of a well-known college for women. She was to address a gathering of alumnae and their husbands in Boston, where she arrived late in the afternoon. To her consternation, she discovered that evening dress was in order.

A violent northeast storm was raging, and the shops were about to close. Making a frantic effort, she managed to collect a dress, shoes, and accessories and to reach her hotel with just time enough to change her costume. Taking a taxi to the hotel where she was to speak, she disembarked so hastily that she fell flat in four inches of slush and water. The hasty ministrations of a maid did little to repair the damage, but she managed to enter the crowded dining room just on time. To her horror, she was the only person in evening dress. She was the only person not informed that because of the storm, the dinner had been made an informal one. She saw at once that the circumstances had conspired to cast her in the role of victim and took advantage of it. Her brief but witty account of her tribulations convulsed the audience and brought her an ovation. Another person in the dean's situation might have been so upset that her speech would have been ruined. Here a lively sense of humor added to the effect of a well-prepared speech.

The art in presenting yourself as a victim consists in making each successive calamity seem to be the last straw—then in capping it with a worse disaster. It is not, of course, necessary to be strictly factual. A little rear-rangement of detail or heightening of drama is permissible to make a better story. But economy both of detail and of wording is essential. If the story is going very well, you may be tempted to ad-lib in order to prolong the effect. This is a mistake; you should leave the audience hungry for more. A similar effect can also be achieved in a much less elaborate form. A simple remark, whether true or not—"That is a subject I failed twice in college" —may form a bond with each member of the audience who ever failed a course during his academic career.

The Apt Quotation

A second way to inject a light touch at an appropriate moment is to use an amusing *quotation*. English litera-ture—not to mention world literature—has an imposing array of satirists, iconoclasts, and wits from whom you may draw apt citations to enliven your speech. In the course of a talk on "Efficiency and the Computer," a commencement speaker was warning his audience against losing sight of an issue by concentrating exclu-sively on statistics. He brightened his point by citing G. K. Chesterton's remark that "Man is a biped, but fifty men do not make a centipede." Later he quoted the same author in establishing the point that praise for one aspect of a project or person does not necessarily extend to the whole: "If a man shoots his mother-in-law at a range of five hundred yards, he is a good shot, but not necessarily a good man." Quips of the same nature may offer amusing support or contrast to a point you are making.

Oscar Wilde has long been a source of brief quotations since his wit was turned in many directions. "The value of an idea has nothing whatever to do with the sincerity of the man who expresses it" and "The only thing to do with good advice is to pass it on. It is never of any use to oneself" are reasonable examples of the economy and bite of his phrases. An Anglo-American writer known for his wit, Logan Persall Smith has a store of observations such as "There are few sorrows, however poignant, in which a good income is of no avail" and "What is more enchanting than the voices of young people, when you can't hear what they say?" Ambrose Bierce, Mark Twain, H. L. Mencken are American writers who could turn a sharply humorous phrase, and you may find in them a storehouse of quotable remarks, one of which may provide you with an apposite touch of humor to charm and relax your audience.[1]

Incongruity of Word or Situation

Perhaps the best and most pervasive way to employ humor is through clever or *unexpected wording* or *incon-*

[1] An excellent collection of illustrative anecdotes, proverbs, legends, definitions, and aphorisms, arranged by professions, is now available. It may well save you the effort of time-consuming research. The title is *The Modern Handbook of Humor*, edited by Ralph L. Woods, published by McGraw-Hill Book Company, New York, 1967.

gruous combinations of ideas. If your talk is formal in its nature, you may insert an extremely colloquial word in an unexpected place. The opposite process will work in an informal speech. No one was a greater master of the unexpected but well-chosen word than Mark Twain. Consider this passage in which Twain is discussing the overwhelming ambition of boys in Hannibal, Missouri, to be steamboatmen:[2]

> We had transient ambitions of other sorts, but they were only transient. When a circus came and went, it left us all burning to become clowns; the first Negro minstrel show that ever came to our section left us all suffering to try that kind of life; now and then we had a hope that, if we lived and were good, God would permit us to be pirates. These ambitions faded out, each in its turn: but the ambition to be a steamboatman always remained.
>
> *Life on the Mississippi*

Here both the unexpected word and the incongruity are combined. The words *burning* and *suffering* provide a gentle but mounting exaggeration. They have emotional overtones which are incongruous. But the climax is reached when Twain applies a *good* life and *God's permission* to a career in piracy. Here the humor is an integral part of the wording of the passage. The humor plays around the text without altering its essential meaning.

E. B. White provides another fine example of the two techniques employed at the same time. He is considering

[2] Mark Twain, *Life on the Mississippi,* copyright 1944 by the Mark Twain Company.

a text on how to improve one's writing. The unfortunate author of the text had used the word *personalize*. Mr. White comments: "A man who likes the word 'personalize' is entitled to his choice, but we wonder whether he should be in the business of giving advice to writers. 'Whenever possible,' he wrote, 'personalize your writing by directing it to the reader.' As for us, we would as lief Simonize our grandmother as personalize our writing."

Mr. White's use of the words *lief, Simonize,* and *grandmother* not only constitutes high humor, but it will make the reader pause before *he* uses *personalize*. Mr. White's technique is a confirmation of Horace's remark which heads this chapter.

Poets must weigh words with special care. Hence when they wish to create humor, they too depend upon precise wording and the juxtaposition of incongruous images. When Dryden was attacking the poets who were his contemporaries, he chose Shadwell as his principal target. He is speaking in the voice of Flecknoe, "the Prince of Dullness"

> Shadwell alone, of all my sons, is he,
> Who stands confirmed in full stupidity.
> The rest to some faint meaning make pretense,
> But Shadwell never deviates into sense.

The words *faint* and *pretense* put the rest in their proper place. But *deviates* is a masterly word as Dryden uses it. Not even by an accidental wandering from his intent can Shadwell be lucid. This humor is too savage for normal use, but it does indicate how powerful is the right word in the right place.

A lighter, more playful, humor which still makes a very sharp point is found in Alexander Pope's work. He uses precisely the same techniques: exaggeration, the balance of incongruous ideas, and very careful selection of words. Her lover has just clipped a curl from Belinda's hairdo for a keepsake:

Then flushed the living lightning from her eyes,
And screams of horror rend the affrighted skies.
Not louder shrieks to pitying heaven are cast,
When husbands or when lap-dogs breathe their last.

Pope keeps a perfectly straight face. But he presents the wide gap between cause and effect, and the equation between husbands and lapdogs makes a serious social comment, ridiculous as it seems on the surface.

Humor as Seasoning, Not Substance

Like all good things, humor is subject to abuse. Your primary function as a speaker is to inform your audience. If you can entertain them in the process, you have gained a great deal. But too much entertainment detracts from the substance and weight of your speech as a whole. A paraphrase of Addison's announced purpose in the *Spectator* provides a useful rule of thumb for a speaker. Addison said that he proposed to season seriousness with wit, and to temper wit with seriousness. The more skillful you are in employing humor, the more carefully you should place it. It should relieve the seriousness of the audience, not the seriousness of your subject matter. The audience should not let your important points slip by while they wait for the next amusing remark.

But by selecting key areas of your speech to season with humor appropriate both to your nature and the nature of your topic, you will make your speech more palatable to your audience. Indeed, a touch of humor may make an important point memorable. But most important, it brings you and the audience closer together. It can warm a cool audience and captivate a friendly one.

Chapter 15
SPEECH OF INTRODUCTION

Whenever people gather to hear a speaker—at a convo-
cation, a department meeting, or a dinner—someone
must present the speaker or speakers to the audience.
That person has the serious responsibility of composing a
speech of introduction which should be both gracious
and informative. It establishes the tone of the occasion.
A thoughtful, well-prepared introduction is the least a
speaker deserves for his expense of time and effort in
preparing his remarks for the gathering. It should open a
corridor of communication between speaker and audience and should establish an immediate rapport between
them.

The chairman, or master of ceremonies, has one
cardinal rule to remember. The audience came to hear
the speaker—not the chairman. Therefore, his introductory remarks should be brief. Three minutes should
suffice for a normal introduction; however, if there is

only one speaker or if his background is of unusual interest, the length may be extended to a maximum five minutes. Brevity on the part of the chairman is a testimony to his good sense and modesty. It reflects his desire to establish a frame in which the talent and personality of the speaker will show to full advantage.

Gathering Information

The very fact that a speech of introduction should be brief makes it difficult to compose. If the chairman does his job properly, he will gather material about the speaker from as wide a range of sources as possible. Since he wishes to open lines of communication between one individual and a group of individuals, he should try to gather information from family, friends, and associates, as well as from the speaker's record of achievement. That record is probably familiar to most of the audience. But it is the little known, personal experiences which will make the speaker warmly human in the eyes of the audience. The chairman's task, then, will be to exercise a careful selection, a balance between subjective and objective material, and to adjust his material to the time he has set for himself. He will have to reject much that he would like to say, to exercise a strict editorial blue pencil in his wording. If he succeeds, he will have a stirred audience and a grateful speaker.

In gathering his material, then, the chairman should not depend on *Who's Who in America* or a resumé prepared by the organization represented by the speaker.

His associates and friends will be glad to supply information about his human qualities and interests, perhaps with colorful anecdotes to illustrate them. His wife is an excellent source of the human interest which warms an audience toward a speaker. Of course there is on record one wife who was approached for information and who replied: "I have been married to David for seventeen years and I haven't found anything very interesting in him myself."

However, most wives will be less frank and more inventive. If none of his sources is sufficiently productive, the chairman may have to resort to a story involving some member of the speaker's profession, a story which will stress the human aspect of the profession. What is important is that the speaker be presented as a personality, not as a collection of statistics.

The speech of introduction, in its common form, falls into one of four categories: *Who's Who in America,* vague generalities, qualifications of the speaker, the characteristic anecdote. The examples which follow may be slightly exaggerated, but experience suggests that some of them have been heard far too often.

Who's Who in America

This is the commonest type of introduction, usually derived from a resumé prepared by the speaker's office or from a publicity release. It begins with the speaker's place of birth and proceeds through his educational career from the nursery to a possible Rhodes scholarship.

The audience is then treated to a roster of degrees, honors, clubs, and a chronological sketch of the speaker's progress from office boy to chairman of the board.

It is a great privilege for me to introduce the main speaker of the evening. He was born in Litchfield, Maine, where he attended the local schools. Upon graduation from the local high school, he went to Harvard University, where he received his B.A. degree, majoring in English. After Harvard he received his master's degree from Columbia. He then served two years in the Marine Corps and was commissioned a lieutenant. When his stint in the service was completed, our speaker spent two years at Oxford University. Upon completing his work at Oxford, he returned to this country to take a position with the Hallex Corporation starting as director of sales training. Within two years he became assistant to the president and on last July was made president of the corporation. Our speaker is a member of the Congregational Church, is active in community affairs, and is a three handicap golfer.

It gives me great pleasure to introduce to you Mr. James Trast, president of the Hallex Corporation, who will speak on "The Future of Computers in Business."

This is hardly an imaginative introduction. It sketches in a perfunctory way what the speaker has done, but it gives no hint of the man's personal qualities. It does not touch on the qualities which make him interesting and important as an individual; it creates no bond between him and the audience. An introduction of this type hardly reflects credit on the one who makes it. Obviously he has made little effort to honor the speaker or to stim-

ulate the audience. He has regarded his task as a chore—
not an opportunity. No bond has been established between audience and speaker, who must now try to arouse
a group whose interest has been dulled.

Vague Generalities

This type, unfortunately, is almost as common as the
Who's Who, but it lacks whatever merit that category
may have, namely, concrete accomplishments—however
trite or however inappropriate to the occasion they may
be. Here there is simply a mass of platitudes and broad
unsupported statements. This form of introduction suggests that the chairman has made no preparation at all;
it is as great an affront to the speaker as introducing him
by the wrong name or wrong title. This type goes somewhat as follows:

> We are most fortunate tonight to have as our guest
> speaker a man who was chosen as the number one citi-
> zen of his city only last year. He has taken great interest
> in civic affairs. He has contributed greatly to the devel-
> opment of new business in a city hurt by the loss of its
> textile mills and its textile industry. He is the author of
> two books. He is widely regarded as a teacher. He has
> taken special interest in the new art museum. He has
> made startling discoveries during his archeological jun-
> kets to Egypt. He was cited last year by the President of
> the United States.
>
> It is a great honor to present to you this evening a
> very versatile person who is devoted not only to his
> community but to his lovely wife and four daughters.

Rather than the generalities contained in this example, it might be well to know *why* he was chosen as the citizen of the year. If he has taken great interest in civic affairs, *what* interest did he take? If he has contributed greatly to the development of new business, *how* did he accomplish this? If he has taken special interest in the new art museum, *what* was the special interest? If he has been cited by the President of the United States, *what* was the citation? There is nothing wrong with mentioning several of the accomplishments of the speaker, but the list should contain specific information.

The Qualifications of the Speaker

I am sure that you share my sense of honor in having Jim Stark as our speaker this evening. Having served for ten years on the faculty of the Massachusetts Institute of Technology, he was asked by the President to serve as a special adviser to the Atomic Energy Commission. Professor Stark was one of the first Americans to visit Hiroshima after the historic atom bomb had devastated the city. Subsequently he spent several years making an intensive study of the physical effects of radioactivity on the survivors.

Last year he was one of eight scientists to visit Bikini, this time to study the psychological effects of an atomic detonation. The results of this study are to be published in ten languages and are to be sent to every nation of the world.

I am proud to present Professor Stark, whose subject is "The Conflict between Atomic Energy and Man."

This introduction provides some of Professor Stark's background through specific experiences in events of great significance. It is easier for the audience to infer his qualifications from these concrete experiences than from a listing of his degrees, publications, and memberships on committees.

The Anecdote

There are times when a story can reveal more about the speaker than mention of his talents and accomplishments. The record books, newspapers, and magazines can supply a wealth of information about Ted Williams, the former great but controversial star of the Boston Red Sox. Yet these statistics and opinions may not be as significant of the man as his visits to children afflicted with cancer in a hospital which he helped to support. The human side of Ted Williams affects an audience more than a recitation of facts and figures—most of which are reasonably familiar to the audience.

Here is an example of an anecdote used to introduce a speaker who might well have been presented under any of the other categories:

> Seventeen years ago a young boy playing in the Boston railroad terminal was severely injured in a train accident. He was rushed to the City Hospital and within hours both his hands were amputated. The newspapers carried the headlines of this tragedy the following morning. A short time later our speaker, after reading this announcement, visited the hospital and asked the receptionist if he could see the young lad. The recep-

tionist replied that the head surgeon had left explicit instructions that only family members could be admitted to his room. As our speaker started to leave, the receptionist noticed that he had two claws for hands and immediately recognized him as the man who had played in the movie *The Best Years of Our Lives.* She called him back and said that it would be all right for him to go into Jimmy's room. Mr. Russell went into the room where the boy was lying and without so much as a word began to take off his coat, untie his tie, and unbutton his shirt. He then reversed the whole process, manipulating his claws with great skill. When he had finished, he looked at Jimmy and said, "I lost my hands too; I lost them in the war. I think you can see that I can get along almost as well as any man with the use of two hands. When you are ready, I will see that you get the same equipment that I have, and I'll also see that you are taught to use your new hands."

At this time I present not only a great actor but a great human being, Mr. Harold Russell.

At the Democratic Convention in 1956 Mr. Russell was given the usual introduction provided for speakers on such occasions. Had this anecdote been used instead, there is little doubt that the 1,500 people present and the 60 million television viewers would have been deeply moved. The simple story says more about the speaker's stature as a person than a succession of adjectives or statistics.

Another introduction employing a single, characteristic anecdote was used effectively to present a recent commanding general of the United States Marine Corps. It is short, yet it places emphasis on specific and outstanding human and professional qualities. The chairman here shows great skill in his selection of material and in keeping himself in the background. He does not once use *I*, *my*, or *me* in his introduction.

It is an honor to have General Chester Puller, United States Marine Corps, Retired, here to address us this evening.

General Puller is affectionately known to Marines throughout the Corps as "Chesty." This nickname is more than an abbreviation for Chester—it is a summary of this Marine's character and is an indication of how his men regarded him.

A page out of General Puller's career demonstrates why this label is so fitting.

The time was 1942—the place, Guadalcanal. General Puller, then a lieutenant colonel, was in command of a regiment driving inland after having established a beachhead. He was leading his men across a clearing in the jungle when it happened.

The Marines were advancing cautiously across the open ground when suddenly Japanese snipers opened up from the trees on the other side of the clearing. The combat-experienced men dove to the ground to find what cover they could. Colonel Puller remained standing amid the crackling sniper fire and shouted to his men in an effort to get them moving and into a relatively less dangerous spot: "Move out! They can't hit you!" He had barely finished when a sniper's bullet hit home and knocked him off his feet. Rebounding immediately, Chesty called to his men: "Hell, when they hit you, they don't hurt!"

This is the way Chesty Puller always ran his operations—up front with his troops and with vigorous aggressiveness. The Navy Cross is the second highest award for bravery in the Naval Service; Chester Puller won four of them.

It is indeed an honor to have this man as our guest. General Puller."

Some Common Errors

Finally, the chairman should avoid other pitfalls which are all too common. First, he should not impinge upon the speaker's subject matter. In his enthusiasm, the chairman may prepare himself not only on the speaker, but on his topic. By failing to confine his remarks to the speaker, he spoils the main speech and earns the just resentment of the speaker. Second, he should avoid such deadly clichés as "The speaker needs no introduction" (why introduce him then); "I give you"; or worse, "I give you none other than . . .";, "Without further ado." Such tired expressions reveal that the chairman has not given thought to his wording. And third, the chairman should introduce the speaker to the audience, not the speaker to himself. Since the speaker's name is probably on the program or has been generally announced, there is no special merit in withholding it from the audience until the end of the introduction. When the chairman presents the speaker to the audience at the end of his introduction, he should face the audience as he does so. Then he may turn to the guest of honor, summon him by name, and wait for him at the podium. This technique is most important when there are several speakers. The audience may know who is to speak, but they may not be able to identify the individuals sitting on the platform.

The speech of introduction offers an unusual challenge to the person delivering it. If brevity is the soul of wit, it is also the essence of the introducer's art. Within the few minutes at his disposal, he must show that he has taken his assignment both as a compliment and as an opportunity. He can acknowledge the compliment by a fresh, imaginative introduction which will reflect the scope of his sources and his good taste and judgment in selecting the material he uses. He can meet the opportunity by preparing the audience to be warmly responsive to the speaker. His surest guideline will be to put himself in the speaker's place—to ask himself, "In what way would I like to be presented to *this* audience on *this* occasion?"

In the process of developing the points you propose to make in your speech, you may run into difficulty. One or more of your crucial ideas will prove to be complex or far removed from the common knowledge of your audience. You are placed in a quandary. To develop the point verbally you will throw your speech out of proportion. You must make the point clear, but to do so will require too much time and too tedious an explanation. In this contingency a visual or audio aid may solve your problem perfectly.

A new and imaginative industry has sprung up to solve in fresh and original ways just such problems as confront a speaker who must make long, labored explanations. The audio-visual industry has multiplied and refined both mechanical and electronic apparatus designed to demonstrate, to explain, to illustrate. Furthermore, new and effective techniques for employing these apparatus are constantly being developed. Industry, advertising, education, and science itself are making increasing use of the materials the audio-visual industry is producing and perfecting. Many of these may be of significant value to a speaker.

Of course some of the material is not new; it has simply been improved. The blackboard is almost as old as education. Colonial schoolboys did their exercises on slates. And even today in impoverished areas of the world for example, the Arabic Near East, students work algebra problems with a piece of chalk on the rough surface of a macadam road. The proprietor of the old medicine shows had gaudy charts to show the situation before and after the victim dosed himself with Indian Snake Oil or Peerless Painkiller. The Chatauqua lecturer stood before a crude screen with a clicker in his hand or a pointer to thump the platform as a signal to change the lantern slide. Today the blackboard is likely to be green —for better visibility. The charts may be sophisticated overlays to illustrate a developing theme. Slides in brilliant Kodachrome are projected on an iridescent screen by remote control from the speaker's platform.

But there is also an almost unlimited variety of new media. There are inexpensive motion pictures which can show a process in slow motion and stop the action at points of special interest. Filmstrips provide a step-by-step description of an action from the movement of a piston in a motor to the change from bud to seedpod in a flower. A wide selection of projectors makes it possible for a speaker to choose one which will show vivid, multi-colored sketches and diagrams or will annotate previously prepared sketches as he speaks. Another projector permits him to reproduce a page from a book or periodical. The plastics industry has provided ingenious models in infinite variety by which the speaker can bring a detailed, concrete image before the eyes of the audience. Many of these models can be broken down into their component parts. A heart surgeon explaining the insertion of a plastic valve to a lay audience might well find a model of this sort extremely useful. He should not count on the audience's vague memories of secondary school courses in physiology to make his references intelligible. All these are essentially visual aids, but there are audio aids as well.

The refinement of tape recording makes it possible to use citations from speakers, eyewitness reports, the give-and-take of a panel discussion, the sound of an industrial process, the song of a bird, or a passage of music with an immediacy and point lacking in a secondhand report. Speakers seldom resort to taped material, but if you are quoting from a speech by Winston Churchill, it will produce a more vivid effect to have Churchill speak for himself than to attempt to imitate his rolling periods. The possibility of using sound to enhance your speech should not be neglected.

But this wealth of audio-visual material involves the speaker in certain hazards of which he should be aware. Like all good things, these aids can be misused. Unless you are a professional speaker, you have neither the time nor the background to make yourself expert in all the available media. Each one has its special techniques; each has its own limitations. Failing to understand them may detract from the effectiveness of your speech, rather than increase it. Another hazard is more serious. What the speaker has to say, his conviction, and the force of his personality must dominate the speech. If the situation is reversed and the device becomes the focus of interest, then the speaker is reduced to a secondary role; he becomes a disembodied commentator. There is a world of difference between a speech and an illustrated lecture. A travelogue is a perennial source of entertainment, but the principal interest of the audience lies in what they see, not what they hear. A speech is the reasoned, informed conviction or persuasion of a person whose views are the prime source of the audience's interest.

Selecting the Appropriate Aid

Your first problem, then, is to decide whether some form of visual aid will actually improve your speech. As you organize it, you may decide that at one or more points a visual aid will be a vivid and forceful substitute for a tedious explanation. Since more people are eye-minded than ear-minded, a clear picture or diagram may make the point far better than a three-minute technical exposition. A visual aid performs its function when it clarifies or explains a specific point more quickly and more tellingly than words. If you conclude that an aid will carry out this function in your speech, then you must decide which of the aids at your disposal will best accomplish your purpose.

Different media will be effective with different audiences. A committee advocating an urban renewal project in an old New England seaport had to convince two divergent groups that its plan to renew—not destroy—the existing business center was advantageous. The historically and esthetically minded group was persuaded through the skillful use of color slides. These established that the buildings threatened with demolition represented authentic Federal architecture which other historic cities had preserved and restored at great cost. The evidence placed before their eyes convinced this group and gave them renewed pride in their town. For the other group—the hardheaded realists—the committee prepared a motion picture to show what restoration had done for the prosperity of Williamsburg. Without ignoring the charm of the restored buildings, the film stressed the crowds of visitors, the busy inns and motels, the thronged restaurants and shops. The appeal of the film to the business community was immediate and practical. In this instance the committee used different media to appeal to different audiences with equal success.

Even within one medium, however, the kind of audience may determine what type of apparatus is best for the speaker to use. A person giving a talk on skiing to a mixed audience would use film with both sound and color and would include romantic shots of Alpine scenery, of people singing around a fire after a day on the slopes, of quaint buildings—as well as sequences of spectacular runs. His object is to catch the atmosphere of the ski resort as well as the grace and skill of expert skiing. On the other hand, a ski instructor would use black-and-white film and a projector which could be both stopped and reversed. His purpose is to teach; so he requires an apparatus which will analyze both good and faulty techniques, an apparatus which will stop a movement at a critical point. Both men are interested in a single subject; both men use the same basic medium. Yet within that area they select from the range of possibilities the one kind of apparatus which will be most appropriate to their purpose and to their audience.

There is another important consideration in selecting your visual aid. You must select one which is suited to the room in which you will speak. Nothing annoys an audience more than not being able to see or hear something to which the speaker is calling attention. If, then, you are to speak on some aspect of atomic power and you have planned to use a model of a particular reactor, you may find that the auditorium is so large that only half the audience will be able to see the model clearly. However attractive and accurate the model may be, you should abandon it and substitute a slide or a projected diagram which will be easily visible to the whole audience. You can control the form your visual aid will take, you can seldom control the place you are to speak. Failure to consider the size of the room may leave you with a restless, dissatisfied audience. Furthermore, if you are using a screen, its size and position, the type of projector which can produce a clear image at the required distance, the power of the amplifiers and their location, and the availability of electrical outlets are logistical problems which cannot be left to chance. Julius Caesar is quoted as saying that when he learned that his great rival,

Pompey, always allowed for the element of chance in his planning, he knew he would win the Civil War. If you have devoted much time and effort to preparing a fine speech, its success should not be marred by the neglect of simple, practical detail.

There are one or two further ways you may go astray if you do not consider the size and shape of the room in which you will be speaking. If you propose to use charts or diagrams which will be thrown on a screen by an overhead projector, are you sure that the detail on the

Chart Too Small. The chart illustrated here is too small to be effective. People sitting only a few feet away would be unable to see any detail. Holding the chart as he does here, the speaker cannot draw attention to its features without obscuring it further.

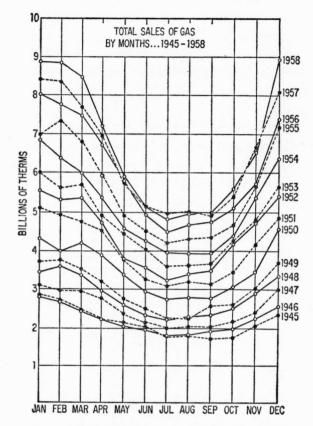

Chart with Thirteen Lines. A chart should make its point simply and directly. It must be clear to even the most distant member of the audience. The mass of intersecting lines in this chart helps neither speaker nor audience.

charts and diagrams is distinct from the back of the room and from the sides as well? Charts overcrowded with detail may be incomprehensible to the more distant portion of the audience—who are not likely to be attentive to an explanation of what they cannot see. If you propose to use a blackboard, you must again be careful to make your diagrams and handwriting clear to those in the rear seats. Before selecting this last device, you might ask a candid friend how legibly you write on a blackboard.

Should you be in a quandary as to what device will best fulfill your purpose, or as to what model is the most appropriate, you would do well to consult a professional in the audio-visual industry. If he were to suggest an overhead projector, for instance, he might also be able to produce a set of overlays. These can be produced in a

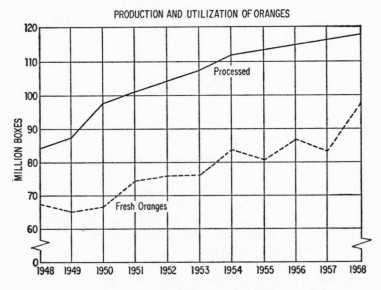

Chart with Two Lines. This chart is simple enough to make its point quickly and well. The speaker can refer to it with ease.

variety of colors and so arranged that they can adapt to a process either of synthesis or of analysis. This device has been so successful that it is utilized in a number of the latest textbooks. Furthermore, the overhead projector has the added advantage of functioning in a fully lighted room.

Casting Light on the Subject

Light is most important to you. You should not, ideally, be a voice heard in the darkness while the audience fixes its attention on a brilliantly lighted screen. If you are to control your audience, you must be visible. There may be times when you gain so much by showing a few slides or a fragment of a motion picture that a momentary darkening of the room is well worthwhile. But the basic principle can be illustrated by the experience of the vice-president of a New York corporation who was addressing a group of employees on the merits of a revised pension plan. As a visual aid, he used comparative charts thrown on a screen by a slide projector. Although the room could not be darkened completely, the figures on the screen were sharp and distinct. But there was sufficient light for the audience to see the speaker. His vigorous, animated presentation of the plan gripped them and won their enthusiastic support. A little later on he gave the same talk to another group— this time in a completely darkened room. But the audience remained relatively unmoved. The explanation was simple. In the first place he was a vibrant human being, communicating with his fellows; in the second instance he was a disembodied voice speaking to an audience whose attention was directed to a screen—not to him. Whatever visual aid you employ, therefore, you must stand in sufficient light so that you maintain close personal touch with your audience.

It may seem that mentioning some of the hazards and pitfalls inherent in visual aids would make a speaker hesitant to use them. Such is not the case. When they are well used, they are supremely effective. When they fail, it is not usually because they were poorly chosen, but because one or more minor details were overlooked. You must remember that what is routine for the expert is not routine for you when you use audio-visual equipment only on rare occasions. Like an airplane pilot, you should prepare a check-off list so that no neglected minor detail will spoil an otherwise triumphant effort. A little foresight and organization may save you from making embarrassing apologies to your audience.

Operating the Equipment

In some instances, of course, you will not be operating the equipment yourself, but on other occasions you may well have to be both speaker and operator. Your first move, then, should be to have thorough instruction in how the device works; next you should practice with it until you have confidence both in the apparatus and in yourself. Fortunately most audio-visual equipment is very simple to operate, but the time spent in practice will mean that you can concentrate on your speech without being distracted by nagging doubts about your equipment. Still you need a check-off list to assure yourself that no untoward accident will disturb your poise in the period just before you are to speak. Many of the items on a good list will seem to be either trivial or obvious, yet experience has shown that more difficulties stem from minor details than from major items. It is easier to forget an extension cord or the take-up reel on a projector than the projector itself. Everyone has experienced the wild, last-minute flurry when some minor but essential piece of equipment proved to be missing or of the wrong type. You might pretty much concentrate your checklist on the minor logistical problems.

Your list may simply be a set of appropriate questions. Where are the electrical outlets, and what voltage do they carry? A burned-out machine will call for instant revision of your speech. If the equipment carries a three-pronged plug, have you a converter? Most older buildings will not have suitable outlets. Is extension cord necessary, and how much? Is the proper kind of screen available or must you provide your own? If you are using a projector, have you a spare bulb—and can you make the change? Have you confidence that you can control tone, volume, focus, in the machine you are using? Can you adjust film or slides rapidly? Have you arranged your material so that you have everything in its proper order so that you do not have to search for items and so that you do not have to turn your back to the audience? If you plan to use a pointer, is one available and is it long enough? It is questions of this nature which will form a list that can be quickly checked, but that will set your mind at rest once the check has been made.

Charts and Blackboards

The emphasis thus far has been on projectors of one kind or another. Charts and blackboards have been mentioned in passing, but actually they are perhaps the most frequently used of all visual aids. It would be difficult to imagine a school or college classroom without a blackboard because it is an invaluable aid in clarifying explanations. But like projectors, charts and blackboards may be used well or ineffectually. It is easy to assume that suggestions and warnings about their use are merely a matter of common sense. So they are. However, minor errors in technique can do disproportionate harm to an otherwise well-organized, persuasive speech.

It has already been suggested that the audience must be able to see the detail on the chart or the material on the blackboard. But *when* the audience sees either one, is also important. Proper timing is essential in a speech. Therefore material on the charts or blackboard should not be exposed to the audience until the moment you plan to use it. Until that moment comes, these aids should be covered. If they are not covered, the audience will tend to speculate on their significance rather than to devote their full attention to you. Furthermore, when you do turn to them, you have lost your sense of climax. The audience will have anticipated much of what you propose to say. The blackboard presents a further problem. If you attempt to write on the board during the course of your speech, you must either stop speaking or else speak with your back to the audience. Neither alternative is good. Therefore material on the board should be written prior to the speech, or if you must write or draw as you talk, you might consider using an overhead projector so that you can face the audience. Indeed blackboards, charts, and magnetic boards should be so placed that you face the audience as you direct their attention to the material you display. Here, too, consideration for your audience should dictate that you use a pointer. Using your finger or arm will obscure the material for at least part of the audience.

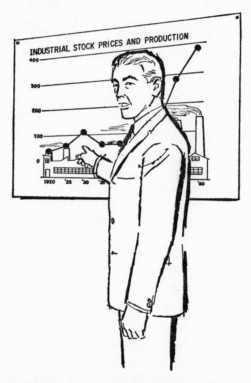

Standing in Front of Chart. A chart which seems to make an important point is obscured by the speaker. By using a pointer he can face the whole audience and expose the entire chart to their view.

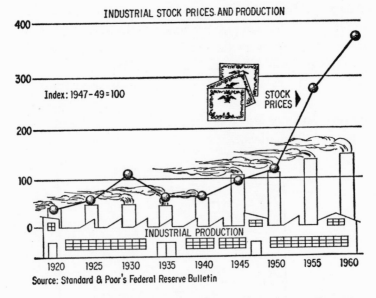

INDUSTRIAL STOCK PRICES AND PRODUCTION

Index: 1947-49 = 100

STOCK PRICES ▶

INDUSTRIAL PRODUCTION

Source: Standard & Poor's Federal Reserve Bulletin

Smoke Stacks. This is another chart which should be simplified for a speaker. The audience may have their attention diverted from the statistical material by the imaginative artwork. Imaginative treatment belongs to the speaker here—not the artist.

Although charts are among the best visual aids, they have their special problems, too. The chief of these is excessive complexity. You may be tempted to crowd too much material on one chart. Several simple, clear charts shown in succession are almost always more effective than a chart which attempts to be too comprehensive. To display a chart or charts, an easel is probably the best device. It can be placed where it is visible to the audience and convenient for you. It may easily be covered until you wish to display the first chart. An easel avoids the insecurity involved with thumb tacks or tape which sometimes give way at the wrong moment.[1]

The Lectern and the Manuscript

Two additional items may be included as visual aids: the lectern and your manuscript. These differ from the other aids because they are of more direct benefit to you than to the audience. But properly combined and arranged, they permit the audience to see you at the same time that you see what you are reading. Therefore you

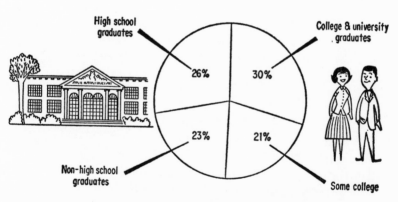

SHAREOWNERS ARE DIVIDED
AMONG ALL EDUCATIONAL GROUPS

High school graduates — 26%
College & university graduates — 30%
Non-high school graduates — 23%
Some college — 21%

Pie Chart. A pie chart is an excellent device for showing relative numbers or relative sizes. The pictures of students and a school building, however, are simply distracting.

[1] A very useful and informative book on charts is the *Graphic Charts Handbook*, by Anna C. Rogers, published by Public Affairs Press, Washington, D.C.

GROWTH OF SHAREOWNERS IN PUBLIC CORPORATIONS

Source: N.Y.S.E.

Chart with Funny Faces. A chart is effective for a speaker when it focuses attention on specific facts. In this chart the eyes of the audience would be drawn to the faces rather than to the statistics which support the speech.

should learn whether the lectern can be adjusted to conform to your height. It should be high enough so that you are not forced to drop your head as you read: The top of your head is not your most attractive and expressive feature; so it should not be presented to the audience. Furthermore when you look down, it is almost impossible to enunciate clearly.

On the other hand, if the lectern is too high, you will appear like the Cheshire Cat in *Alice in Wonderland*—a disembodied head! As a result you will be unable to make gestures without waving your arms in the air. The lectern must also be well lighted. You can hardly devote your full attention to your audience if you must peer at your script in an effort to decipher it. You will be much more comfortable in your mind if you know beforehand that the height of the lectern suits you and that there is adequate and soft light. Too much light causes glare and makes you squint.

Your manuscript, when you use one, is *your* important visual aid. It should have the features common to other good aids. It should be extremely easy to read and to handle. Since the art of reading from a text is to give the impression that you are speaking directly to your audience and not reading at all, your manuscript should be designed to contribute to that impression. It should be expertly typed on a machine which has a large, bold,

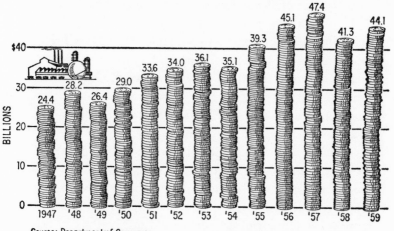

BUSINESS IS INVESTING MORE MONEY IN PLANTS AND EQUIPMENT

Source: Department of Commerce

Stacks of Gold Coins. The stacks of coins are an invitation to the audience to let their imaginations roam. A clear, simple bar chart would be more useful for a speaker.

plain typeface. It should be triple-spaced for ease in reading and so that you may make last-minute changes or notes to indicate special stress. The easier your script is to read, the less often you will have to drop your eyes to it. So you will maintain better eye contact with your audience. The manuscript should be on fairly heavy paper for ease in handling. Thin stock tends to flutter, to wrinkle, and to stick together. For the same reason, it should be carried flat in a portfolio—not folded. Then when you speak, the text will lie flat on the lectern, and you can slide each sheet to one side as you finish it. This method minimizes handling the script and leaves your hands free for gesturing. It also avoids distracting your audience with a continual flutter of papers and having them speculate on the length of your speech by the visible transfer of sheets from one place to another.

Visual aids as a whole, then, are precisely what the term implies. They are aids—valuable aids. As such they must be kept in their subordinate position. They support oral communication; they do not replace it. One vibrant human being sharing his thought and his feeling with a group of his fellows is still the essence of communication. But the speaker may summon the aid of electronic science to help him project his voice. Through visual devices he may call upon the eyes of his audience to support the appeal to their ears. Again this support is secondary. Since you wish to be as clear, as vigorous, as persuasive as you can be, you should not hesitate to utilize these aids when you can. They can add color, vividness, and concreteness to your words. They give you a new dimension in developing your thought.

Chapter 17
CONFERENCES

Oral communication in conference form has become part of the American way of life. No matter what your business or profession may be, no matter what position in life, or in the community, you hold, it is almost certain that you have been or will become a member of a conference. It is extremely likely that at some time you will conduct one. Like the other forms of oral communication, conferences have their special techniques for the participants and for the leaders. Whether the conference is productive or not usually depends on the skill with which the members and the leader play their separate parts. Of the two, the leader plays the more significant role. For if he is sufficiently skilled, he can train the members to function effectively even while the conference is in progress.

For convenience a *conference* may be defined as a gathering of informed persons for the purpose of collecting information or of reaching a consensus; a *meeting* may be defined as a gathering whose purpose is to provide or disseminate information. A second distinction is that a *conference* is usually limited to a dozen or fifteen members; whereas a *meeting* may consist of a large number of people.

The importance of efficient conference technique can be supported by a few figures. In the June, 1967, issue of *Fortune* magazine were listed the 500 largest industries in the United States, a group which employs over 12 million people. One company with 80,000 employees held 1,100 sessions in its training center for 17,000 men and women. But this figure did not include the impressive number of meetings and conferences conducted in twenty smaller conference rooms. Nor did it include the conferences in its branches throughout the nation and the world. Since the investment represented by the space devoted to conference rooms is not a small sum, the effective use of that space is obviously a matter of major importance. However, the value of the space is secondary to the value of the men who occupy it. Of course the men who are in conference are working, but in most instances they are not engaged in their specific jobs. Hence the man-hours spent in conference represent a far greater investment on the part of industry than mere space does. Six or seven department heads engaged in a two-hour session is an expense which can be justified only if the session is productive. Furthermore, if you multiply the experience of this one company by even the 500 listed in *Fortune,* poor conference technique can be responsible for a most significant financial loss. In business and industry as a whole, the number of man-hours spent in conference raises the possibility of loss to a staggering sum.

Of course business and industry are not the only sources for conferences. Civic and community organizations, professional and educational groups, even purely social organizations may call on you to take part in a conference, or even to lead one. Here, too, you and your associates are asked to give valuable time to pooling information or to seeking the solution to a problem. Again, time is a precious commodity. If the chairman or leader is ignorant of his function or faulty in his technique, he will both waste the time of his associates and ensure that the information gathered will not be definitive, nor the consensus be clear. Likewise the person who has been asked to participate in a conference may fail to make an adequate contribution to the discussion, or may even hinder its progress, because he does not understand his function.

The conference method has been firmly established because the explosion of knowledge makes it impossible for one man to be expert in many fields, because decision as a result of discussion rather than fiat is a part of the American way of life, and because the method offers valuable by-products. As both business and society in general become larger and more complex, men tend to become isolated in their special fields of competence. The conference brings together informed men from different areas to express their views and to explain their problems. The very fact that departmental problems are aired and explained may contribute largely to their solution. In the second place, a conference establishes confidence between different echelons of industry, or between different segments of society. Whether in business or in industry, the lower echelon is assured that upper management is sufficiently interested to seek its help in solving broader problems; hence it gains confidence in the quality of its leaders. Third, the conference method provides an invaluable training ground for prospective executives, since it provides them with an understanding of the functions and problems of a number of departments. Possessed of this overall view, they will be more confident in accepting new assignments.

Types of Conferences

Again for the sake of convenience, conferences can be grouped into two general types. The first of these, the discussion type, will have as its purpose the sharing of information in a defined area so that executives may have information on which to base a decision on policy. The second is a problem-solving type, which directs its attention to the solution of a precise and clearly defined difficulty. In both types the basic purpose is the same— to elicit pertinent information so that a sound executive decision may be reached. However, the problem-solving type addresses itself either to a difficulty or to a proposal whose scope is limited on the one hand, yet touches a number of departments on the other. Actually, the problem-solving type may spring directly from the discussion type. The general discussion may result in a consensus that a policy of reducing inventories should be instituted as soon as possible if only the needs of certain customers can be anticipated and met. The discussion conference thereby raises a problem which a subsequent problem-solving conference must deal with. The personnel involved in each of these two conferences is not likely to be identical. The problem can best be solved by those closest to it.

The function of the conference, then, is to define the problem or the proposal, to establish its cause or its justification, and to suggest solutions for it or means of implementing it. The consensus drawn at the end should indicate what responsibilities each department will undertake. Other types of conference might be cited, which would be subdivisions of these two, but these are sufficient to illustrate proper conference technique.

Preparation for the Conference

Suppose, therefore, that you are required to direct a conference. How should you approach your responsibility? What should you bear in mind if the conference is to be productive? Your experience as a speaker will serve you in good stead here. You have the same obligation to prepare for the conference that you have to prepare for a speech: Your active direction of the conference corresponds to the delivery of the speech. Finally, you must treat the members of the conference as you treat your audience if you are to elicit from them the most thoughtful and enthusiastic contribution they are capable of making. You will be in the position of an orchestra conductor facing a group of skilled but temperamental musicians, each of whom must bring his instrument into play at just the right time, and for just the right duration. Therefore each of these areas, preparation, direction, and personnel, demands careful attention from the conference director.

You may feel that some of the suggestions offered to you are obvious ones. Yet all too often the obvious requirements are neglected just because they are obvious. For instance, a conference must meet somewhere, but you might be so absorbed in the problems to be discussed that you neglect to reserve a conference room for the day and time of your meeting.

The Agenda

Having ensured that you have a place to meet, you then should see to it that each member of the conference receives an agenda well beforehand. A stated agenda allows each participant to collect his thoughts and to assemble the pertinent information and data which will lend substance and authority to his observations. If it is not possible to send out a formal agenda, you might at least suggest the areas to be covered as you invite the members to take part. By so doing you will avoid the difficulty experienced by a sales manager who called a meeting of his representatives on the Eastern Seaboard. One of the core problems was the fact that some of the industry's products were not selling in areas where the potential market was good. He had neglected to send an agenda in advance, and the conference lapsed into an expression of generalities and unsupported opinion because the data upon which a fruitful discussion depended remained in half a dozen widely separated branch offices. Had the representatives known which products and which markets were to be discussed, they could easily have prepared themselves for an informed, authoritative exchange of information which might have solved the problem. The result, however, was a costly gathering which was unable to discuss the difficulty in concrete terms.

Even when you have prepared a fixed agenda, however, you must exercise care in wording the topics or problems to be discussed. Unless the area is clearly defined, many of the difficulties attendant on having no agenda at all may arise. A large manufacturing company recently held a conference in an attempt to solve a communications problem. The broad area of the problem lay in the inadequate flow of information from the shop to the main office. Fifteen department heads were summoned to a conference in the hope of finding a means to improve the situation. The chairman presented the topic for discussion in the following words: "We have a communication problem, and we have called you men to help us find a solution. It has been reported that there is friction in some of our departments which is harming our labor relations."

A discussion lasting an hour and a half produced no concrete results. However, a consensus was reached that the vague wording of the opening statement was responsible. At that point one member recalled that a survey had indicated a lack of cooperation between foremen and first-line supervisors. With a definite area isolated, a second meeting of the same group quickly revealed that the core of the problem lay in the objection of the foremen to merit interviews. With a specific topic to discuss, the conference quickly reached a satisfactory solution. The difference between a vague and a specific agenda was the difference between a futile and a highly productive conference.

Time Is Money

Another important factor in preparing for a conference is the time element. The men you summon to confer are unquestionably men whose time is valuable. It is a minimal courtesy to them that the conference begin on time and end on time. Consequently the agenda must be restricted so that it can be covered in the designated time. If several topics must be considered, you should plan rather carefully the time to be alloted to each one and hold to that time.

Who Should Attend

While you as conference leader cannot be expert in all the special fields which will be represented at the conference table, you must prepare yourself so that you recognize digressions when they occur. Another facet of your role as leader is to see that all pertinent aspects of the problem or policy are covered by the expertise of the men you invite. If a vital area of discussion is not represented, the conference may quickly reach an impasse. The members of the conference may balk at arriving at a consensus or a solution if they feel that an important view is missing. For instance, a question of the strict legality of a proposed course of action might well prevent a decision unless a legal expert were present. As conference leader you should anticipate the trend the discussion will take. Just as a speaker must consider his audience in advance, so you should weigh the characteristics and predilections of the men you invite—as far as you are able to do so. If you are aware, for instance, that the head of one department is not likely to contribute to the discussion or to commit himself to a decision unless he is abreast of the latest findings of the research department, you would be well advised to include a man from research in the conference.

Arranging the Room

Still another important duty is to choose the room, if choice is possible, or at least to see that it is suitably arranged. A small group is usually more comfortable in a small room which tends, in itself, to pull the group together. But the arrangement of the room is even more important than its size. Long experience has shown that a conference is most successful when each person can see every other person without making an effort. Under such circumstances good eye contact can be maintained. As a result each speaker tends to receive the complete attention of the group. For this reason the long table which often adorns a directors' room is not at all suited to a conference. Even an oval table is often not broad enough to permit everyone to see everyone else. The best ar-

(a) POOR ARRANGEMENT

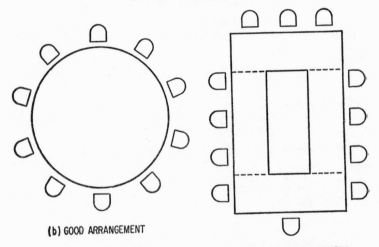

(b) GOOD ARRANGEMENT

(c) EFFECTIVE ARRANGEMENT

Conference Setup. (a). Conferences held at long, narrow tables lose much of their effectiveness because the members have difficulty in seeing the person who is speaking. Each speaker, then, tends to address his remarks to the leader rather than to the group as a whole.
(b). For a small conference a round table is an ideal solution.
(c). By placing tables more nearly in a square, the difficulties in the long table are removed. Each participant can see each of his colleagues and be attentive to him when he speaks.

rangement is a group of small tables which can be arranged in a square, for eye contact is important for each member. A grouping of small tables can be expanded or contracted easily to fit the size of any conference. The unfortunate tendency is for each speaker in turn to direct his remarks to the conference leader. Actually he should address the group as a whole and should focus their attention by maintaining eye contact with each one of them.

With respect to the room, you have additional duties. If the conferees do not know each other well, it is a thoughtful act to have place cards propped up so that everyone at the table may read the names from his seat. Just prior to the conference you should see that pencils and a pad of paper are provided at each place. When visual aids—blackboards, projectors, charts, or samples —are required, you should see that they are in the right place and in working order. All these precautions simply represent your consideration for the members of the conference. Any delays occasioned by your failure to anticipate physical requirements will result either in a failure to cover the agenda or to end the conference on time.

Leading a Conference

However careful your preparation has been, your real test as a conference leader comes during the course of the conference itself. Certain techniques and attitudes prove helpful to experienced leaders, but again you will probably adapt each of these techniques to fit your own personality or the nature of the conference you are directing. However, these techniques form a reminder of the duties you assume as a leader.

In the beginning the leader should establish his role as the iron hand in the velvet glove by setting up ground rules. One of these may be the length of time any speaker can hold the floor. He might set the limit at three or four minutes until everyone has had an opportunity to speak on the article of the agenda which is before the group. By so doing he can cut short, without embarrassment to them or to himself, speakers who tend to go on too long. He should also proclaim his position as referee in determining what is pertinent to the discussion and what is a digression. If he is tactful, he will point out that both ground rules are designed to make sure that there is time for an expression of opinion from everyone who has a contribution to make. The members of the conference will carry out their functions better if they know at the very beginning that their time will be employed efficiently.

Following the statement of the ground rules, the leader should remind the group briefly of the agenda and perhaps indicate how much time should be spent on each part. At this point he can perhaps direct the purpose of the conference to the phase of the problem or proposition which should have special attention. Unless the group is so small that he can perform the function himself, he should designate someone to act as recorder and to take notes on the sense of the meeting. Perhaps the recorder can report a consensus at the end, perhaps not. But the leader should not undertake this responsibility in any except the smallest of meetings, for it is his prime function to keep the discussion lively and directed to the point at issue. Should the conference be larger than a half dozen members, the leader may stand for the opening announcements. By so doing he commands instant attention, and the members are more likely to heed the ground rules he establishes. Furthermore, he at once can establish the effect of good eye contact. At the conclusion of his opening remarks, he sits down for the ensuing discussion.

Your quality as a leader will be challenged at the very beginning of the conference. If the discussion opens in a desultory way, you will find it difficult to provide the impetus necessary to ensure a vigorous, multifaceted attack on the issue before the conference. For this reason you might have two or three members primed to begin the discussion at once. In case of an initial hesitation, you can activate the device simply by saying: "I know that Joe and Frank have some definite thoughts on this situation, and I have asked them to present these thoughts to you."

This stratagem gets the discussion off to a flying start when people are a little reluctant to be the first to speak or when they are collecting their thoughts after your preliminary remarks. A spontaneous discussion should follow.

Another method is to ask each member to speak in turn, but this is less likely to be productive, because the participants are more inclined to think of what they intend to say than to listen attentively to the man who is speaking.

Once the discussion is in full flow, your function is to

make sure that everyone has a fair chance to be heard, that obscure statements are clarified, that digressions are checked, that private conversations between members do not occur, and that the discussion is animated rather than heated.

Human nature being what it is, a small group within the conference may try to dominate it. Should this occur, you exercise your function as leader by saying, "Tom must have some pertinent ideas on this point." By drawing one of the more reserved members into the discussion, others will be apt to follow his lead. A brief restatement on your part will often help to clarify a point which you sense lacks definition in the minds of several members of the group. At the conclusion of the reserved member's observations, you might remark: "As I understand it, Tom, your point is that the bond issue is sound, but that the timing is wrong."

At this point Tom can either accept your summary or be more precise in his conclusion. But in an effort to clarify or to define a point the discussion may wander into problems of technique when the attention of the group should be centered on a question of policy. You must be quick to sense the situation and to correct it. Fair is fair, and if one member is permitted to talk on collateral matters, everyone has a right to digress. Since your position is that of a fair-minded, impartial referee, calling a penalty for the first infraction is the best way to see that the rules will be followed. The same sense of fair play should make you quick to interrupt tête-à-têtes. Each person speaking deserves the full attention of the whole group. Private conversations are distracting to the person who has the floor; so you should not hesitate to ask people to reserve their remarks until the speaker has finished. Finally, should the discussion of a point become too heated or acrimonious, you might shift at once to the next item on the agenda on the theory that more heat than light is being generated. If there is time, you can return to the sensitive point after tempers have had a chance to cool and after you have attempted to reintroduce the topic with a little humor. In fact, touches of humor on your part can keep friction from developing in the first place.

The mention of humor as a means of inhibiting undue warmth suggests the opposite problem—what to do when the discussion cools down too far. Naturally it is your function to see that this drop in temperature does not occur. To prevent it you should have a battery of questions ready before the conference begins. As a referee you must be neutral; you should not influence the discussion nor comment on areas outside your own special field. But a boxing referee must see to it that the men in the ring remain active. So should you. These questions, judiciously used can stimulate a fresh activity in the conference. They fall into two types: the specific and the general.

Specific questions are useful in clarifying a situation and in leading to a conclusion. Often they require a simple, factual answer: "What were our total costs last month?" "Are there any legal problems in the solution as offered?" These questions only occasionally stimulate discussion; but in keeping the collective feet of the conference on the ground, they may suggest a general problem which should be discussed. The general question is a more productive source of stimulation. The use of *why, how, what, when, where,* and *who* will almost ensure a rush of ideas: "Why do you think cutting the advertising budget would be a solution to this problem?" "How would you handle the current dispute with Local 126?" "What is your reaction to this complaint by the Better Business Bureau?" "When would be the most appropriate time to put this plan into action?" "Where do you think we could get adequate financing for a new branch?" "Who can tell us whether our water supply is adequate for the projected operation?" By their very nature questions such as these demand answers which form a ground for discussion. Of course, you cannot anticipate exactly how the thought of the conference will run, but you can reinforce the questions you prepared beforehand with others which occur to you as the conference proceeds.

If you are to move through your agenda in the allotted time, you must occasionally be autocratic. You may have to cut off discussion of one point before everyone is satisfied. But autocracy works here democratically, since finishing the conference on time will be a distinct advantage for most of the members. You should be careful to allow time at the end for the recorder to express the sense of the meeting or the consensus, if the group has arrived at one. It is helpful to send, subsequently, a written summary to members of the conference and to department heads to whom the information is pertinent. You should also save time for a brief word of thanks. People are usually quite willing to make efforts, but they like to feel that their effort is not simply taken for granted. A word of thanks is particularly appropriate when the conference leader is in a position to require that the members be present at the conference.

A good conference can be most productive. If a university should be a cockpit of learning, where opposing ideas and theories meet and clash, a good conference should be a cockpit of talent and skill. Here the give-and-take, even the clash, of opinion is likely to produce new ideas and new approaches to old problems. It unites varied departments and talents in the consideration of a problem or project, so that they gain understanding and respect for each other's skills and demands. Yet none of these impressive results will appear unless the conference has live topics for discussion, is well planned, and is led with imagination and tact.

CONFERENCE INFORMATION SHEET

Subject ....

Conference leader ....

Date ....

Place ....

Length of meeting ....

Was agenda sent? ....Yes..(   )....No..(   ).......

Results of discussion ....

....

....

....

....

Members present ....

....

....

....

To whom was summary sent? ....
....
....
....

A form similar to this one provides a helpful checklist and review for conference leaders. It is also of value to executives and department heads. The summary reassures them that the time of the members was spent profitably and that further information is available to them if they seek it. The fact that all interested people receive a copy may preclude another department's calling a conference on the same material.

You may remember that for the sake of convenience a *conference* was defined as a gathering designed to elicit information and hopefully to reach a conclusion. At the same time a *meeting* was defined as a gathering whose purpose was to provide or disseminate information. In the broad terms of that definition, a meeting may take many forms. It may be the directors' meeting of a corporation, a convention, a meeting of the trustees of a public institution or a university, a lecture, a travelogue, a sales gathering to present new or improved products, a PTA meeting, a forum, or a panel discussion—to name but a few. All these meetings differ from conferences in that the people who attend come to be informed. Not everyone is expected to contribute to the topics which are discussed; not everyone is chosen as an expert in a special area. The flow of thought is outward from the speakers to the audience rather than inward from the participants to the chairman or his deputy, who must record a consensus or announce the solution to a problem.

It is true that a small meeting may resemble a conference in that many of those present may make observations or ask questions. But if the distinction is kept between the directions in which the information flows, the questions and observations in a meeting will simply clarify or amplify the material presented by the designated speakers. Indeed good questions from the floor frequently contribute to the success of a meeting, for they indicate that the attention of the audience has been firmly engaged. They are not, however, essential to the meeting, and by the nature of some meetings, they are not practical. A meeting at which several speakers must present their views in a limited time may not offer an opportunity for questions or comments.

Suppose that you are asked to preside at a meeting or to make the arrangements for one. What are your duties and responsibilities? Obviously the scope of your task will depend on the size and importance of the gathering. But certain fundamentals hold true in almost all instances. In your position as chairman, you may or may not be responsible for choosing the speakers. Even if you do choose them, you cannot guarantee a first-rate performance from any one of them. But you can be sure that the organization of the meeting is smooth and flawless. You can assure yourself that you will not have to apologize either to the audience or to the speakers for mechanical failures which you should have anticipated and prevented.

Setting the Scene

Your first concern should be for the comfort of your audience and your speakers. Since a well-filled hall produces a desirable psychological effect, you should try to estimate the size of the audience in choosing the hall or room in which the meeting is to take place. If you are constrained to use a room larger than the size of the audience warrants, then you should impress ushers into service so that the audience can be gathered into a compact group at the front of the room. Nothing is more disconcerting for a speaker than several rows of empty seats directly in front of him. If no ushers can be found, you should at least urge people to move forward before you begin the meeting.

You should also consider the heat and the ventilation. No one can be very attentive when he is physically uncomfortable. A room which is warm and airy before the audience arrives may be hot and stuffy when it is filled. Someone must be ready at a signal from the chairman to adjust the heat and source of air. The audience may also be uncomfortable if it cannot hear clearly. You should check the acoustics to determine whether a microphone and amplifiers are necessary. If they are you should check again to be certain that those at the back of the room can hear at a predetermined amplification. Cries of "Louder!" from the rear and the subsequent frantic adjustments of a tuner do not conduce to an auspicious start.

Again, you should check on the platform lighting.

One good way to throw a speaker off stride is to fail to provide enough light for him to read his notes. Since even an experienced speaker may be nervous, you should make sure that water and glasses are placed within easy reach of him. These suggestions may be trite, but they are often overlooked just because they are taken for granted. If you check details which contribute to the comfort of audience and speaker alike, you have made a long step in the direction of a successful meeting.

There is one further step to take in preparing the place for the meeting. When you have your speaker or list of speakers, you should find out whether projectors, blackboards, screens, extension cords, etc., will be needed. If a lecturer, for instance, is to show slides or films, there may be some question as to whether he will bring all the necessary equipment or whether he will expect you to provide some of it. Fifteen minutes before the announced start of the meeting is an unfortunate time to discover that a vital piece of equipment is missing, yet this is a fairly common occurrence. A letter or a telephone call beforehand will obviate a possible difficulty. If you are responsible for a sales meeting, you will most likely have to provide space for charts to be displayed or for products to be exhibited. By knowing in advance exactly what is required, you can plan effective displays rather than improvise just before the meeting. When you neglect these precautions difficulties are bound to arise.

A few years ago some three hundred people assembled at a New England college to assist at the dedication of a new building. The ceremony was held in a large and impressive dining hall, one end of which formed a rotunda with tall windows providing a handsome view of lawns and trees. The head table was placed against this impressive background, which in itself would have been distracting enough, especially since the sun streamed in through the windows. But a group of curious children who peered in during the president's dedicatory speech drew the unanimous and amused attention of the audience. Had the person in charge of the arrangements seen to it that the curtains were drawn, he would have provided an admirable background for the speaker. Neglect of one detail spoiled what should have been a memorable ceremony.

Another instance of neglecting to weigh the effect of a physical setup occurred when the vice-president of a large corporation called a meeting of some forty or fifty salesmen to brief them on new products. The room had previously been used for a meeting of the advertising department. The walls were covered with brilliant illustrations from the latest advertising campaign, and a wealth of visual aids were on display. Under the circumstances it was impossible for the speaker to hold the attention of his audience, fascinated as they were by the display. A prior inspection of the room would have revealed the presence of attractive nuisances, and they could have been removed before the vice-president's speech began.

Is an Agenda Necessary?

In addition to the normal preparations, some meetings by their very nature require you to make further efforts. When the meeting is a formal or stated one—a board meeting, a trustees' meeting, a convention, a sales meeting—you will do well to have an agenda in the hands of those who are to attend well before the time specified. If the meeting is as large as a convention, those attending can select beforehand the smaller meetings, panels, or discussion groups they wish to join. A delegation, for instance can so distribute themselves that they take full advantage of what your convention is offering.

Since the agenda for a comprehensive meeting or a convention should be detailed and explicit as to time, place, chairman, speakers, and topics for the smaller meetings which form an essential part of the overall gathering, it behooves you to take particular pains with details. If possible you should check personally to see that the rooms are clearly marked, that they actually will be free at the time you want them, that you have allowed time for a room to be rearranged before scheduling a second meeting in it, that special equipment needed for one room has not been delivered to another by mistake. When you cannot make these checks in person, it is still helpful to have them in mind so that you can at least confer with a deputy who has been asked to make a personal survey. But even a small, formal meeting will profit from an agenda. Knowing what must be covered during the course of the meeting, the participants are less likely to take too long in presenting their reports or in developing one topic on the agenda. Hence it should be as clear and as explicit as you can make it: what officers and committees are to report and in what order; what items of unfinished business remain for disposition; what specific items of new business must be discussed and who will speak on them. With such an agenda in their hands beforehand, the members can gather their thoughts so that their questions and comments will expedite rather than retard the meeting.

Dinner or Luncheon Meetings

A dinner or luncheon meeting presents you with additional problems. Is there to be a head table? Who besides the speakers are to be invited to sit at it? Where are they to be placed? If cocktails are served before dinner, how are people to be lured into the dining room so that a reasonable time schedule can be maintained? Your answers to these questions often mean the difference between a smooth and a calamitous meeting. The more people you ask to sit at the head table, the more will feel indignant and slighted that *they* were not asked. The presence of a large group at the head table takes the focus of attention away from the speakers and may even force them to exceed their time if they feel they must mention the persons who share the table with them. These problems are reduced when you keep the head table small. Committee chairmen and other stalwarts may be rewarded in other ways. But if you are to have a head table, you should arrange the seating so that congenial people are placed next to each other. You must be diplomatic here, for a public as well as a private dinner can be spoiled if you inadvertently place persons of strongly opposed views or sympathies side by side. By using place cards and tact, you can be reasonably sure that the guests at the head table will find both their proper seats and pleasant companionship.

The problem of the cocktail hour really tests your ingenuity. If it goes on too long, or if people are allowed to bring drinks to the table, you are almost certain to have a lethargic and inattentive audience by the time the speakers are introduced. Furthermore the serious drinkers will straggle in late and will not finish dinner in time to have the speaking program begin promptly. You may appoint aides to assist you in moving the group into the dining room at the proper time. Also, you may deem it wise to have the bar closed down fifteen minutes before the announced time for dinner. But you must have some plan if the meeting is to run on schedule. A ground rule about bringing drinks to the table should also be established; otherwise if there is a source available, there will be a stream of diners drifting out to replenish their supply, and you may have to deal with more serious problems than inattention. These precautions indicate the concern you feel for the speakers, whose time and effort deserve an attentive and responsive audience.

There is one final detail you should not neglect at a dinner or luncheon meeting. The audience should be able to see the speaker. But it often happens that the speaker's table is decorated with flowers or an elaborate centerpiece. You should have these decorations removed before the speaker begins. There should be no obstructions—no matter how attractive—between the speaker and his audience.

Establishing Time Limits

At the time speakers are invited to address a meeting they should be given a definite time limit. The time allocated to each should be a few minutes less than his normal share of the time available. Speakers tend to exceed their limit rather than scant it, and since you have probably arranged for the most important guest to speak last, he should have his full quota. A strict and economical time schedule is vitally important when your meeting is to be followed by a luncheon, a dinner, or another meeting. In these instances your meeting must adjourn on time. There is no margin for error unless you build one into the structure of your program. At the morning session of a recent sales conference, there were five speakers listed for the program which had to end promptly at noon because a distinguished guest was to speak at luncheon. The final and most important speech of the morning was to be given by the sales manager of the corporation. He had been asked to present his thoughts in seven minutes, and he had worked hard and long to present a brilliant new concept in that restricted time. In spite of assigned—but too generous limits—the first three speeches were much too long. As a result the chairman had to announce: "I am sorry, but the last two speakers will only have two minutes each in which to express their views." Outraged by this cavalier treatment, the sales manager refused to speak at all.

In this instance poor planning by the chairman resulted in a painful and embarrassing situation. A meeting adjourned a few minutes ahead of schedule may well be most successful; a meeting which runs behind schedule is usually a failure.

A final note on your preparations also concerns the speakers. If one or more of them is coming from out of town, it is a thoughtful act to meet him in person or at least see that he is met and taken to his accommodations. The speaker is thus assured of his welcome and put at ease by attentions which may not be necessary but which are nevertheless gratifying. He will also appreciate being provided with a place where he may be quiet and collect his thoughts for a few moments before the program begins.

Serving as Chairman or Moderator

With the preparations well in hand, you may find yourself with additional responsibilities. Perhaps you are to serve as chairman of the meeting or toastmaster at the dinner in addition to your duties as the organizer and director. It is for that eventuality that the suggestions for organization come first, for it is easy to be so much concerned by your own speaking part in the proceedings that you neglect the routine details of organization upon which a successful meeting depends. Your duties as an active participant in the meeting will naturally depend upon its size and nature.

If you are to serve as the moderator of a panel or forum, your tasks will be very similar to those of the chairman of a *conference*; hence you might check the suggestions offered in the chapter on that topic. There is one important difference, however. Unlike a conference, a forum or panel has an audience present. Hence you must be strict in your impartiality and you must be scrupulously fair in giving divergent views equal time. In addition, the audience will normally be invited to ask questions. Questions from the audience are common at other meetings also; so the suggestions which apply here will also apply to similar situations.

In the first place you might ask the questioner to identify himself or herself. At times the identity of the questioner is of no significance. At other times, the weight of the question will depend upon the person asking it. The president of a bank, a well-known lawyer, the superintendent of schools, or the editor of a magazine or paper may ask a question which is of special import because of the position he holds. If the occasion is a panel or forum, you should also ask to whom the question is directed. In any event, the question should be repeated by you so that all those present may know exactly what it is. Unless there are overhead microphones, those members of the audience seated behind the questioner may not hear what was asked with the result that the reply will lack relevance for them. You must also be quick to cut short those who wish to deliver a speech rather than ask a question. You can do so by interrupting with "Will you state your question please!" At times it may be necessary for you to clarify a question. It may be asked in such a garbled or vague form that an effective reply is impossible. You can rescue both questioner and speaker by clarifying or firming the questioner's wording.

In the event that you are presiding at a meeting where the principal speaker has agreed to answer questions following his talk, it is your duty to announce the fact. The climax of the speaker's address is spoiled when he remains at the podium to explain his willingness to entertain questions. Just prior to closing the formal part of the meeting, you might announce that Dr. Learned will be happy to answer any questions the audience may have. There is a danger, of course, that no one will at once produce a good question—both to the embarrassment of speaker and audience alike. The problem here is the need to break the ice, to give people time to formulate their questions. For this reason you might ask two or three people beforehand to take the initiative in getting the question-and-answer period under way. They may not have to act, but they should be quick to do so if there is any hesitation.

When computers began to achieve major significance, a meeting of bankers listened to a brilliant exposition of the role computers might possibly play in banking and finance. The speaker had offered to answer questions after his formal presentation but none were forthcoming. However, ten minutes later, the intrigued audience had many pertinent queries when it was too late to make them. The men at this meeting needed just a little time to arrange their thoughts so that their questions would be good ones. Had the question period been started by prearrangement, a lively and informative session would have followed. If you as chairman exercise a little forethought, you will not leave to chance a productive and stimulating aspect of the meeting.

Perhaps at this point a word might be said about the technique of answering questions. As chairman or moderator you may have a question directed to you. After you acknowledge the question and repeat it, for you are still the chairman, you should direct your answer to the audience as a whole rather than to the person who asked the question. The essence of a meeting is to spread information; so the general audience is entitled to your views on the issue raised by the question. Furthermore, by directing your attention to the audience, you can quickly recognize another questioner. This technique is especially useful when the first questioner deliberately introduces an unpleasant or strident question. After a brief reply, you can shift the topic quickly if the meeting is not one designed for vigorous controversy.

Your final duty with respect to the question-and-answer period is to bring it to a close. You should be quick to sense fatigue in the speaker, or a lessening in the number of those striving for recognition. At either point you might suggest that there be one more question. It is always desirable to end a session when the audience is eager for more. In timing the end, you must consider the audience as a whole rather than the few eager souls who would ask questions for hours—given the opportunity.

But as chairman or toastmaster you have more important duties than providing an effective question period. The whole movement and tempo of the meeting is largely in your hands. First of all you should start the meeting on time. But in deference to the speakers, you should not begin until the audience is quiet. If a gavel will not bring quiet, you might arrange to have the lights blinked several times. When you have the attention of the audience, you should strictly limit your own remarks. It is your duty to introduce the speakers—not to hold forth yourself. Both audience and speakers will be grateful if you stick to your proper function. Part of that function is to persuade the audience at a dinner meeting to move their chairs so that they face the speakers. No one likes to speak to people whose backs are turned, and circular groups are likely to carry on private conversations. Then you should present the guests seated at the head table. By so doing you at once satisfy the curiosity of the audience and return the focus of attention to the speakers where it belongs.

As chairman or toastmaster the atmosphere and continuity of the program are in your hands: You are the first to speak, you introduce the speakers, you provide the transitions between speakers when there is more than one, and you bring the meeting to a close. Like a frame you give picture boundaries and definition; like background music you create an atmosphere. But you do not thrust yourself into the picture personally; you do not play a solo. You are not competing with the speakers; you are presenting them. Needless to say you will attempt neither to anticipate what they are to talk about nor to summarize what they have said. Your job is to be brief and gracious in your opening and transitional remarks and in your introductions as well. Unless you have exceptional talent, you should not vie with professional toastmasters or masters of ceremony. Few amateurs can compete with professionals in any field. Overambition on your part may well leave the speakers with an audience which is casting surreptitious glances at their watches. Your best plan is to be yourself—your genial, humorous, and most normal self. By so doing you will ensure the gratitude of the audience and of the speakers. You will demonstrate your conviction that the meeting should move forward at a pace that holds the audience's interest and your awareness that the spotlight should be on the speakers.

This atmosphere should be maintained to the very end. Hence you should plan your final, brief remarks with special care. Simply to rise and declare the meeting adjourned is a rather ungracious way to end the proceedings. Even if custom demands that the meeting be brought to a close by a benediction or by a song, a concise but warmly worded tribute to audience and speakers alike will send both away feeling pleased with themselves. A very few carefully chosen words from you can put the final stamp on the impression you have created all through the meeting.

Parliamentary Law

When you are called upon to preside at a formal meeting, you must have some knowledge of parliamentary law or the meeting will fall into disorder. Since few laymen can claim mastery over Robert's *Rules of Order*, you will probably need an easy and convenient guide to lead you through the intricacies of motions, amendments, and precedence. Fortunately such a guide is available: *Group Leadership Manual*, by O. Garfield Jones, published by Appleton-Century-Crofts, New York. It is designed to show at a glance the order in which motions and amendments must be submitted by proponents and the order in which they must be submitted to vote. It also shows which types of motion take precedence over others.

Without some such guide even an experienced moderator may fall into error. An inexperienced presiding officer may lapse into complete panic. Since a calm, deliberate, assured manner is the mark of a good moderator, your confidence will be increased if you have a clear, authoritative, easily consulted code of procedure instantly available.

As a presiding officer you must win the confidence of the meeting as a whole and of the individuals who comprise it. Your understanding, your ability to think on your feet, your consideration for others, and your sense of fairness are all being tested. When you meet this test successfully, few roles will give you greater satisfaction or be more rewarding.

To be asked to organize a meeting or to serve as moderator or chairman is a compliment to you. It is at once an honor and a responsibility. It is a congenial error to think first of the honor and then of the responsibility. But there is very little honor in arranging a meeting or in presiding at one when it is not a success. Since meetings rarely fail because the whole idea of holding a meeting was a mistake, it follows that faulty organization or ineffectual chairmanship is the common cause for dull and unproductive ones. Your invitation, then, is a challenge to you to accept the responsibility and let the honor come as it may. People are quick to distinguish between a smooth-running, well-planned meeting at which the speakers have been a disappointment and a meeting at which fine speakers have been harassed and thwarted because there was no order in time, place, or equipment. If you do your part well, you will bring audience and speakers together in comfort, in as pleasant an atmosphere as you can manage for both, and within the designated time limit. When you do these things, you well deserve both the honor and the compliment.